Cricket Match played at [...]

First In[nings]

No. in order of going in	Name of the Batsman	Figures as Sco[red]		How Out	By Whom	Runs
1	Tiger			Bowled	Smyth	
2	Bullocky	1235131		Bowled	Buller	11
3	Cuzens			Bowled	Buller	0
4	Red Cap	11562		Bowled	Buller	13
5	Mullagh	12114511...		Bowled	Buller	45
6	Lawrence	321/331/3311/		Bowled	Fellows	31
7	King Cole	241		Run out	—	7
8	Dick a Dick	44		Ct & Bowled	Buller	8
9	Twopenny	24		Bowled	Buller	6
10	Peter	2		Bowled	Smyth	5
11	Dumas			Not out		0
	Byes	52122221				18
	Leg Byes	111				3
	Wide Balls	11111				7
	No Balls	111				3
					Total 1st Innings	185

Runs at the fall of each Wicket	1 for 1	2 for 6	3 for 29	4 for 43	5 for 114	6 for 126	7 for 136	8 for 168	9 for 175	10 for 185

Australian Eleven — Second Innings

No. in order of going in	Name of the Batsman	Figures as Scored		How Out	By Whom	Runs
1	Tiger			Bowled	Smyth	0
2	Dick a Dick			Bowled	Buller	0
3	Red Cap	221		Ct Alix	Buller	5
4	Cuzens	12121132221		Ct Bathurst	Smyth	21
5	Lawrence	1		Run out		1
6	King Cole			Bowled	Smyth	0
7	Mullagh	3533		Ct Downe	Buller	12
8	Twopenny	3		Bowled	Smyth	3
9	Peter			Ct Trevor	Smyth	0
10	Dumas			Not out		0
11	Bullock			Absent		
	Byes	1				1
	Leg Byes					
	Wide Balls	1				1
	No Balls					
		Total of the two Innings			Total Second Innings	44

Runs at the fall of each Wicket	1 for 0	2 for 0	3 for 8	4 for 9	5 for 13	6 for 51	7 for 14	8 for 40	9 for 45	10 for

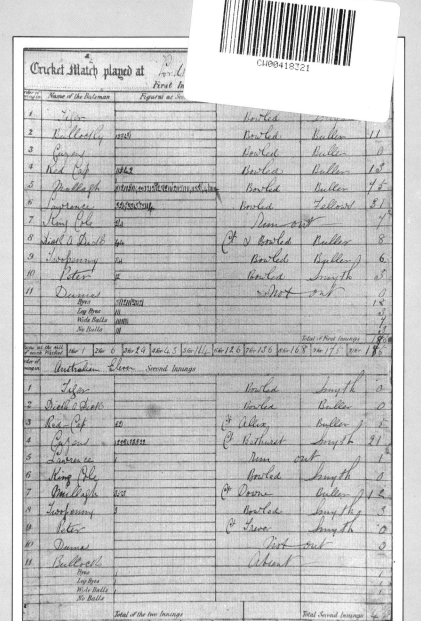

CRICKET WALKABOUT

CRICKET WALKABOUT

**The Australian Aboriginal Cricketers
on Tour 1867–68**

JOHN MULVANEY
REX HARCOURT

M

in association with the
Department of Aboriginal Affairs

First published 1967 by Melbourne University Press

Revised edition published in the United Kingdom 1988 by
MACMILLAN LONDON LIMITED
4 Little Essex Street London WC2R 3LF

Associated companies in Auckland, Delhi, Dublin, Gaborone,
Hamburg, Harare, Hong Kong, Johannesburg, Kuala Lumpur,
Lagos, Manzini, Melbourne, Mexico City, Nairobi, New York,
Singapore and Tokyo

ISBN 0-333-47036-2

Set in Plantin by Graphicraft Typesetters Ltd.
Printed in Hong Kong

Front jacket illustration: The first Aboriginal cricket
team, December 1866. (*Australasian News.*)
Back jacket illustration: Portrait of Nannultera, 1854.
(*National Library of Australia.*)

Contents

List of Illustrations
PLATES

1. The first All-England XI, 1861-62. (Mitchell Library, Sydney.)

2. Arrival of the first All-England XI at the Cafe de Paris, Bourke Street, Melbourne, December 1861. (Mitchell Library, Sydney.)

3. Melbourne Cricket Ground, 1860. (La Trobe Library, Melbourne.)

4. Portrait of Nannultera, 1854. (National Library of Australia, oil on canvas, 99 x 78.8 cm, Rex Nan Kivell Collection.)

5. First international match, MCG, New Year's Day 1862. (La Trobe Library, Melbourne.)

6. Aboriginal cricketers, South Australia. (Robert Edwards and the Royal Geographic Society of Australia, South Australia.)

7. Aboriginal cricket team, Deebing Creek, Queensland, 1894. (Queensland Museum).

8. Aborigines at cricket, Point Macleay, South Australia. (The Godson Collection, Public Library of South Australia.)

9. Cricket match at Coranderrk Aboriginal station, Healesville, Victoria, *circa* 1877. (F. B. Smith).

10. 'The Invincibles', New Norcia, Western Australia, *circa* 1879. (West Australian Newspapers Limited).

FIGURES

Foreword

It was with a great deal of pleasure that I accepted the invitation to write a foreword to this revised edition of the book by John Mulvaney and Rex Harcourt on the first major sporting event of its kind in Australia's history — the 1868 Aboriginal cricket tour of England.

This is more than another book about cricket. It is a commentary on social attitudes; a commentary on the relationship between Aboriginals and Europeans in the 1860s. John Mulvaney's background as an historian and Rex Harcourt's knowledge as an archivist equip them well to write on this subject and they do so with sensitivity and objectivity.

After reading this book one can only admire the courage and the skills of what the authors describe as 'natural sportsmen'. Not only did the Aboriginal team play cricket in England but they also participated in specially arranged sporting carnivals in which they demonstrated their exceptional skills to the English sporting public.

The folklore of Australian cricket began with this tour. The Aboriginal cricket team provided some of the first Australian cricketing heroes who, until the publication of the first edition of this book, did not receive the recognition they deserve. Sadly, even now, very few Australians are aware that the first Australian cricket team to tour England was Aboriginal.

This book is one of the first works of its kind relating to an Aboriginal sporting event. It details precisely and accurately the success of a remarkable group of bush cricketers from Western Victoria who took on England's best.

Cricket Walkabout is a valuable contribution to both cricket literature and Aboriginal sporting history.

I commend it to you.

Charles Perkins

Acknowledgments
for First Edition

Many people assisted in the making of this posthumous tour record; they cannot all be thanked here. Basic information and helpful advice were offered freely by Dr Diane Barwick, Department of Anthropology, Research School of Pacific Studies, Australian National University, Canberra; Mrs Luise Hercus, Australian Institute of Aboriginal Studies Research Fellow in Linguistics, University of Adelaide; and by Mr Hugh Field, Ringwood, the historian of Victorian cricket.

Others who provided assistance of diverse kinds are as follows: Mr L. J. Blake, Melbourne; Mr D. A. Casey, Mt Macedon, Victoria; Mr T. P. Dobson and Mr Jack Cato, Melbourne; Mr D. Edgar, Harrow, Victoria; Mr R. Edwards, Curator of Anthropology, South Australian Museum, Adelaide; Mr F. W. Hayman, Melbourne; Mr Ian Johnson, Secretary, MCC; Mr H. G. Martindale, Cobram, Victoria; Mr R. F. Mulvaney, Melbourne; Dr F. B. Smith, Canberra.

The staff of the La Trobe Library, Melbourne, assisted in many ways, as did Mr H. Nunn and his staff of the State Archives of Victoria. Thanks are due also to Miss C. Kiss, Librarian, Australian Institute of Aboriginal Studies, and to the Librarian, Glenelg Regional Library, Hamilton. Mr P. E. Felton, Superintendent, and the Victorian Aborigines Welfare Board, permitted me to use records which had been abstracted by Dr Barwick.

Miss L. Kopp typed the manuscript with discrimination, and other members of this department who assisted materially with illustrations were Miss W. Mumford, Mr W. R. Ambrose and Mr R. L. Lampert.

In England, the Curator of Lord's, Miss D. Rait Kerr, supplied me with information and illustrations. I acknowledge my debt to her and the trustees of that celebrated ground. The editors and staffs of the following newspapers combed their files for me, and thus compensated for the dearth of English newspapers in Australian libraries: *Daily Telegraph, Sporting Life, Sunday Citizen* (for *Reynolds News and Sunday Citizen*), London; *Derbyshire Advertiser* (for *Derby Mercury*); *Guardian Journal* (for *Nottingham Guardian*); *Liverpool Daily Post* (for *Liverpool Echo*); *Newcastle Journal and North Mail* (for *Newcastle Daily Chronicle*); *Rochdale Observer; Sheffield Telegraph; Telegraph and Argus*, Bradford; *Yorkshire Gazette and Herald*, York; *Yorkshire Post*, Leeds.

It was a cricketing enthusiast from Rochdale, Mr Jack Golson, Department of Anthropology (Prehistory), Australian National University, who ensured that this book was written.

I am also indebted to the staff of Melbourne University Press for patient and efficient assistance.

John Mulvaney

Acknowledgments
for Second Edition

We never would have attempted this expanded version without the initial generosity of two supportive barrackers: Sydney cricket immortal W. J. (Bill) O'Reilly, who donated the accounts ledger kept during the 1868 Aboriginal tour to the Melbourne Cricket Club, and Ian Friend of Ocean Grove, a descendant of 1868 captain Charles Lawrence, who made available family papers. Ian Johnson, the then Melbourne Cricket Club Secretary, granted us permission to consult the ledger and to use other facilities. We also are grateful to Alan Chegwyn and members of the MCC Library staff; other MCC officials and staff assisted us in many ways.

In the Western District, we acknowledge assistance from Mr S. Sondhu, Mullagh station, and Mr D. Edgar, Nerrinyerie station, Harrow; Mrs S. Officer, Mount Talbot station, Toolondo; the late Mr C. Halahan, Edenhope; Mr L. Hill, Mount Gambier.

Assistance from other Australian sources was supplied by S. M. Ingham, Department of History, Monash University; A. P. Fleming, Wollongong; Ms G. Blades, Department of Human Movement Studies, University of Queensland; the Librarian, Benedictine Abbey, New Norcia, Western Australia; John Knott, Woollahra, Sydney; C. Winning, NSW Cricket Association Librarian; the Protocol Officer, Town Hall, Sydney; Roger Page. Dr Luise Hercus, Faculty of Asian Studies, Australian National University, generously made available her own research material. Other descendants of Charles Lawrence, Jerry, Jack and L. C. Leech, of Cairns, supplied an hitherto unknown scorebook. Assistance is acknowledged from the office of the *Bendigo Advertiser*; the staff of Edenhope High School; the library staff, Australian Institute of Aboriginal Studies; and the Mitchell Library, Sydney.

Assistance in England facilitated research considerably. In particular we thank Peter Wynne-Thomas, librarian of the Nottinghamshire County Cricket Club and secretary of the Association of Cricket Statisticians, whose deep knowledge of the sources for cricket history proved invaluable. Help also was provided by Stephen Green, Curator, Marylebone Cricket Club, Lord's Ground; J. Scott-Browne, Secretary, Surrey County Cricket Club; H. A. Osborne, Librarian, Sussex County Cricket Club; F. G. Peach, Derbyshire County Cricket Club. Sir Peter Hayman, Checkendon, Berkshire, advised one of us concerning his family history over a delicious meal of trout.

Typing was undertaken by Jean Whitmarsh while John Mulvaney was visiting Harvard University, where Mrs E. McIsaac also assisted the project. At the Australian National University, the work was completed by Helen Nicol and Sue Nolan. Mandy Mottram drew the maps and Bob Dowhy produced many of the photographs.

John Mulvaney and Rex Harcourt

Preface

Bullocky was absent 'without a satisfactory reason' on 13 June 1868, when the Australian Aborigines started their second innings at Lord's. Without its opening batsman, the team collapsed before the Earl of Coventry, Viscount Downe and the other officers and gentlemen representing the Marylebone Cricket Club. Although they had compiled 185 runs in their first innings, and Lieutenant-Colonel Bathurst twice failed to score against them, the Aborigines lost by 54 runs. This memorable game was played a decade before the first white Australians took the field at Lord's, and 14 years before a mythological cremation created 'the Ashes'.[1]

Bullocky's bizarre pilgrimage to Lord's began on 16 September 1867 when, with 12 Aboriginal team-mates, cook, coachman, English captain and Australian manager, he rolled out of the western Victorian hamlet of Edenhope, in 'a large American waggon drawn by four horses, supplied with tents and "tucker"'. That night their wagon bogged on the track. However, even the continuous rain during their eight-day trek to the coast at Warrnambool, under 250 kilometres distant, failed to dampen the team spirit for nocturnal hunting forays after possum and kangaroo.[2] Charles Lawrence, their 'new-chum' captain and coach, cheerfully adapted himself to the conditions and joined the hunters.

The team made an auspicious entry on to the field to open its Victorian tour. At Warrnambool it scored 140, and then twice dismissed the 16-man European side for a total of 43 runs. Their exit from the colony was even more auspicious.

They proceeded in leisurely fashion from Warrnambool to Geelong, playing cricket at Mortlake *en route*. After the second of their two Geelong matches against the Corio Club, and before supposedly resuming their Victorian tour, they drove to Queenscliff on 22 October for a fishing holiday. A brief game concluded at Queenscliff, they went fishing near the entrance to Port Phillip Bay. On the same day the coastal vessel *Rangatira*, 460 tons, sailed from Melbourne. Off Queenscliff the Aboriginal anglers boarded her and, as steerage passengers, they were spirited out of the colony.[3]

The Aboriginal composition of the first Australian cricket team to tour abroad and its unorthodox departure merit emphasis. Sporting writers over the past century frequently have referred to the tour, but they have shown little inclination to probe beyond superficialities; their colourful copy is studded with errors. Even before the team sailed there was heated debate in the press concerning the origin of the Aborigines' proficiency at cricket and the identity of their mentors. In later years, memories proved fallible so that reminiscences telescoped incidents from two separate tours. The first attempted overseas tour, a few months before this second episode, succeeded only in reaching Sydney. Under these circumstances, selective sampling of the evidence has resulted in misunderstanding. Strangely, some of the most newsworthy aspects, such as their departure, have remained unknown. Regrettably, this team was ignored by the promoters of the 1977 Centenary Test. The public therefore remained unaware that Aboriginal cricketers were the first Australians to play at Lord's, although a letter in *The Times* of London informed British readers of that fact.[4] The tour remains largely unmentioned in more recent surveys of the history of cricket. Even R. Bowen's *Cricket: A History of its Growth and Development Throughout the World*, a wide-ranging survey, dismissed the team cryptically and without elaboration with the comment that, 'in 1868 Australian Aborigines toured England; in 1878, white Australians'.[5]

The tour has been dismissed as a 'curiosity', little better than a vaudeville turn, by some serious students of the game. If their only knowledge of the tour was derived from popular journalism, this conclusion is not unjustified. Such a judgement ignores many factors, some of them of considerable historical interest. Most writers have abstracted the tour from its context in the evolution of the game of cricket, but this is misleading. Aboriginal playing standards must be assessed by comparison with those of their white contemporaries and within the rules and ground facilities of a century ago. This study does not attempt a match-by-match account of the tour, but explores other significant issues which go beyond the confines of the cricket boundary.

This is a neglected episode in race relations, and the origins and aftermath of the tour deserve attention. It had repercussions for Aboriginal administrative policy within the colony of Victoria. At the same time the team's success provides some insight into attitudes of settlers to the people whom they had displaced. The widespread interest in cricket evinced by a generation of Aborigines represented an interesting adjustment to their changed circumstances and requires explanation. At the international level, the tour occurred at a remarkable period in the debate upon man's place and status in nature. This was the decade of the American Civil War, with all its ramifications for concepts of racial superiority or the equality of man. In intellectual history, it was the period of biological controversy generated by Charles Darwin and T. H. Huxley. Evolutionary theories were crystallized in their *Origin of Species* (1859) and *Man's Place in Nature* (1863), respectively. Subsequent years were to convert Australia into a museum of fossil culture and a storehouse of evolutionary facts for Darwinian propagandists. Would the arrival of black cricketers during the evolutionary controversies provoke any scientific comment or public reaction in Britain?

Another less academic but vitally human reason for this

study is to rescue a dignified episode in race relations from oblivion. Aboriginal people should feel pride in the success and character of these versatile Victorian ancestors. It is an object lesson for other Australians that, instead of contempt and prejudice during the nineteenth century, respect and tolerance towards Aborigines could have achieved a more positive interaction and helped to ameliorate generations of suffering and bitterness.

The first edition of this study was published in 1967, at a time when few historians bothered to write about sport and kindred social institutions in a serious manner. Since that time, literature on the sociology of sport, particularly in the nineteenth century, has explored issues relevant to the context of the Aboriginal tour. Another reason for rewriting and expanding the story of the team is the existence of two vital sources of information, unknown in 1967. The first is the discovery of the financial ledger kept during that tour. W. J. (Bill) O'Reilly, a memorable name in cricket history, set an example of public spirit when he donated the ledger to the Melbourne Cricket Club in 1978. More recently, Mr Ian Friend and other descendants of Charles Lawrence, who coached and captained the Aboriginal team, have made available to the authors some valuable papers, including Lawrence's handwritten autobiographical notes, written around 1916, when he was aged about 86 years. Because these new sources add precision to the earlier account, and because they add a personal touch, making some individual cricketers into men of character and great dignity, it is important to make the evidence available.

Readers who compare the texts of the two editions will find that the second one is considerably expanded. Errors and assumptions have been corrected where necessary but the story remains basically the same. It tells of a significant episode in race relations, involving some of the original Victorians in a little-remembered saga.

The original title of the book has been retained. In their

traditional life, Aborigines shifted camp according to seasonal food and water availability, or because of the obligations of ritual life for kin to participate in ceremonial activities. Consequently, they 'walked about' their traditional lands. These practical reasons for periodic shifts in residence bore no relation to the misguided European notion that the Aboriginal mind is subject to some instinctual and overpowering urge to 'go walkabout', regardless of existing obligations. This is racialist nonsense. As the subjects of this book moved from town to town during a two-year period for the practical reason of playing cricket, it seems appropriate to term this international circuit a 'walkabout'.

NOTES

[1] The Lord's match was described in *The Times*, 13 and 15 June 1868, from which the comment on Bullocky is taken.

[2] The team's Victorian progress is described in more detail in Chapter 4. This version draws upon the Melbourne *Australasian* (*Aust.*), 5 October 1867, 428, and *Hamilton Spectator* (*H.S.*), 9 October 1867.

[3] The evidence for the team's unorthodox exit is reconstructed from *Aust.*, 4 November 1867, 62; *Age* (Melbourne), 24 October 1867; *Sydney Morning Herald* (*S.M.H.*), 2 October 1867 and 4 November 1867, 4.

[4] D. J. Mulvaney wrote to *The Times* on 17 March 1977 concerning Aboriginal priority. He was invited subsequently to talk on the subject on the Third Programme, BBC.

[5] R. Bowen, 1970, 118, made no other reference to the team.

1

The Critical Decade

Australian international cricket had two strange benefactors: a Melbourne catering firm and an English novelist. The enterprising Bourke Street restaurateurs Spiers and Pond, determined to enliven a society satiated with gold, and to divert surplus wealth to their own pockets, proposed a 12-month reading tour by Charles Dickens throughout the colonies. When Dickens rejected their lucrative offer of £10,000 potential profit, the disappointed promoters turned their attention from culture to sport, and the less expensive business of arranging an All-England XI cricket tour led by H. H. Stephenson. Their arrival on the *Great Britain* was welcomed by decorated ships in the harbour and the team was lionized by Melbourne crowds who cheered their coach and eight greys along Bourke Street in the manner of royalty. More than 15,000 spectators crowded into the Melbourne Cricket Ground to watch their opening game on New Year's Day 1862 and to quench their thirst from the 500 cases of beer provided (Plates 1, 2 & 3).

Judged by later standards, the cricketing calibre of the tourists was mediocre. However, it sufficed to overwhelm the undisciplined but deferential colonial opposition. It was a social tour, as the number of refreshment pavilions in contemporary illustrations of the MCG testify. Yorkshire batsman Roger Iddison assessed colonial essentials with his complimentary observation: 'Well, Oi doant think mooch of their play, but they are a wonderful lot of drinking men.' Significantly, the captain of the Melbourne team was George Marshall, the publican of the Cricketer's Arms.

To facilitate their identification, the English players wore distinguishing coloured sashes and hat ribbons, the colours being listed on the score cards. Messrs Spiers and Pond also catered for the uncertainties of the game because, should play finish early, paying patrons needed entertainment. Predictably, the Melbourne XVIII was dismissed in its second innings early on the fourth day, when 10 of the team failed to score. The resourceful sponsors consequently staged an ascent of the first balloon manufactured in the colony as an added attraction for their patrons. The two male and one female balloonists cleared the trees with panache and floated to earth in front of the governor's box, before ascending for a cross-country drift to East Melbourne. Such spectator statistics and entertainment facilities are relevant to the later promotion of the Aboriginal tour. So, also, was the knowledge that the promoters made a profit of £11,000 on the tour. Spiers and Pond substituted a notable restaurant in London's West End for the Café de Paris at Bourke Street's top end, while each English tourist sailed home in a first-class cabin, with £250 in his pocket.[1]

Stephenson brought with him six members of the Surrey team which he captained. They included the two men who would infuse skill into Australian cricket, William Caffyn and Charles Lawrence. This All-English XI left England at an important period in cricketing history, a decade during which W. G. Grace was to establish his legendary status. In his autobiography, Grace dubbed this time cricket's 'most critical period', during which drastic action was taken to tighten the rules of the game, improve ground facilities and curb inter-club jealousies. Grace, and later historians of cricket, considered that the firm actions taken and improvements introduced determined the future pattern of cricket.[2] Certainly these changes represented a victory for conservatism, or traditional amateur control by the gentry, over what had become during the 1850s a working-class-dominated and professionalized game in which spectator entertainment and gate takings became important factors. The Aboriginal tour needs to be assessed within this dynamic perspective.

The professional approach typified by the All-England XI, who played continuously and depended upon revenue from gate money, had its origin in 1846. Astute William Clarke then paid his team members £4 each to challenge teams of 18 or 22 men around the country; he prospered on the balance of the takings. These itinerant professionals were drawn largely from the ranks of self-employed working men, artisans and mechanics with some technical skills. The growing railway network enabled them to travel rapidly between fixtures. Their paying crowds lived in the new industrial cities, where improving living standards and reduced working hours enabled many favoured urban workers to afford the time and the entrance fee to become spectators. Publicans were prominent in arranging fixtures and, not surprisingly, they provided all refreshments at a ground, while also accommodating the visiting team at their inns. When reporting matches, newspapers frequently complimented the innkeeper for the quality of his refreshments or his ground arrangements. It is relevant to hostelry profits that professional players often drank heavily, Yorkshire players being notorious in this regard. If drinking was one of their off-field pleasures, playing simple practical jokes upon fellow team members seems to have been another. These were rough, independent, hard-drinking men from proletarian backgrounds, who set a pattern of behaviour which would impinge upon the Aboriginal cricketers.

There was a moderately successful professional tour of Canada and the United States in 1859 which formed the prelude to an Australian cricketing bonanza. Within England around this time, market demands also enabled breakaway teams to elude Clarke's monopoly of the circuit. One such XI was organized by Fred Caesar in 1862, while the United South of England XI, the last major competitor, was formed in 1865. Charles Lawrence formed an All-Ireland XI. Under this rugged system teams sometimes boycotted others and schisms were rife. This free enterprise commercialism climaxed with the second Australian tour of 1863–64, led by George Parr. Each participant received £475 and his travel costs, although 'the money-grabbing of this side helped to delay further tours until 1873'. The Aboriginal team's Australian circuit during 1867 helped to fill the entertainment gap.

Apart from these touring fixtures, most cricket clubs were small social groups, while club teams were scratch affairs, often consisting of volunteers who happened along. The quality of play was not high and it depended upon the quantity of alcohol consumed as much as upon the abilities of the players. Before the 1870s there were some county fixtures, but they were sporadic.[3]

It was literally a far cry from the few thousand noisy spectators at an All-England XI match to the gentlemanly and largely private social encounters of earlier cricket, when talented professionals were retained by noblemen or private clubs. There were many who considered that, unless the upper class resumed control of the game, the sport would lose its social significance and the established moral order would be overthrown. Anthony Trollope, the novelist, was one of these conservative critics. Those who remember the invective and dire predictions about cricket's future when Packer World Series cricket fostered the cult of the individualist may be unaware that history was undergoing repetition. In 1868, the very year of the Aboriginal tour, Trollope fulminated about the mercenary state of the game:[4]

…even cricket has become such a business, that there arises a doubt in the minds of amateur players whether they can continue the sport, loaded as it is with the arrogance and extravagance of the professionals.

In Trollope's opinion, 'the so-called England Elevens, which go caravaning about the country playing against two bowlers and twenty duffers for the benefit of some enterprising publican', was not cricket. It was no better in Australia, he considered, where English 'adventurers' found 'fair fields for earning fresh honours and fresh money'. In sentiments foreshadowing latter-day critics of World Series Cricket, he complained that professionalism was 'the monster cricket nuisance of the day', while players unreasonably demanded special conditions.[5] (H. H. Stephenson and his Surrey teammate Julius Caesar did strike for the 1855 season, when a pay increase was refused by their club.)[6] Even at Lord's, Trollope regretted, 'the Marylebone Club, unable to endure the dictation of their own servants, are compelled to lose the services of men who have on that ground won all the honours on the prestige of which they now trade'.

It is likely that many Marylebone Cricket Club members shared Trollope's opinion of commercial cricket and the dangers of the breakdown of the social order, and the committee initially opposed the Aboriginal team's appearance at Lord's. However, the circumstance of the team's match on that hallowed ground are better deferred for subsequent discussion. Trollope's concept of real cricket presumably involved amateur gentlemen only. Such a person was Lord William Lennox, who watched the Prince Regent (George IV) bat. As an army staff officer in 1815, under the Duke of Wellington, Lennox also played cricket near Brussels, 'about a month before the grand match between Wellington and Napoleon at Waterloo'.

Is the perception of true cricket simply a question of values? Consider another episode recalled by Lennox.[7] This exotic cricketing incident from those Regency times involved the outlay of a heavy bet on the outcome of a single-wicket contest. (Doubtless Trollope would not have condemned this form of aristocratic financial professionalism.) It concerned Lord Charles Kerr, who successfully wagered 50 guineas that his servant, Bridger, and his spaniel, 'Drake', could defeat Mr J. Cock and Mr Wetherall. Bridger batted first and made 50 runs; while the dog was not credited with any score, 'instead of "not out", we may say "never in"'. Cock made only six runs for the opposition and Wetherall was out without scoring. 'Drake' retrieved the ball so quickly that Bridger ran out Wetherall, appropriately under the circumstances, for a duck.

W. G. Grace may have possessed a personality as individual as Lord Charles Kerr, but he proved a vital figure in assisting the restoration of traditional patronage and cricket management by the gentry through the dominance of the county system and the MCC. With a side fielding Grace, any amateur team could hope to better the performance of the mercenaries, an important asset in reasserting control of cricketing arrangements and diverting patrons. Grace played first in 1864. During the period to 1881, there were 40 major fixtures played between Gentlemen and Players, of which the Gentlemen won 27 and lost only five encounters. County clubs increased from 25 in 1860 to 37 by 1870 and the regular crowd-drawing county championship competition started soon after. Under the emerging county system, there was room for compromise, under which a place was found for the professionals who were employed as coaches and ground bowlers, while their rates of pay were higher than those offered by the original entrepreneurs, such as Clarke. By 1885, MCC leadership was unchallenged, its membership numbering up to 3000 and its income £15,000.[8]

The Aboriginal team of 1868 therefore arrived at the close of the heyday of professional exhibition cricket. By the next decade, the professional circuit, aiming only to lure and to entertain paying crowds, had degenerated into troupes of clown cricketers, while the quality of county matches and the magic name of W. G. Grace sufficed to draw crowds with a genuine interest in the sport. A century before the electronic and sartorial gimmicks of World Series Cricket, such exotica were anticipated during the 1870s by Treloar's 'circus', whose eight cricketers paraded alongside eight clowns and eight acrobats.[9]

It is significant that the Aborigines arrived in England just when the rules and practice of the game were in a state of flux. Until this period, cricket fields were no more than their name implies, while wickets were totally unprepared. Sir Pelham Warner relates how a flock of sheep was grazed at Lord's for a day or two before a match, in order to trim the grass. Cattle grazed on the Perth ground in Scotland, where the youthful Charles Lawrence removed grass tufts before even practice became possible. An authority described the Turnham Green sports field upon which the Aboriginal team played as 'a dreadful one all ridge and furrow'. Nottingham's batting pride, Richard Daft, termed pitches as 'simply frightful', while Grace commented that the 'principal grounds were so rough as to be positively dangerous'. Under such conditions, the longstop became the most important fieldsman.

Lord's was no exception. The Sussex team declined to play there in 1864 because the ground was unduly rough, and it was said that the ground's only resemblance to a billiard table was in its pockets. That was the year in which the first groundsman was engaged. While the virtues of ground care and wicket preparation became accepted slowly, most grounds upon which the Aboriginal tourists played would not be acceptable to most village teams today. Only two weeks after the Aborigines played at Lord's, W. G. Grace batted on the same pitch which he recalled was 'very bad'. Indeed, during a match there in 1870, the ball pitched on a stone and struck a Nottinghamshire batsman on the head, killing him. Foreshadowing modern protective helmets, the incoming batsman, Richard Draft, wound a towel around his head.[10]

The greatest revolution in rules concerned bowling. Since the eighteenth century, four-ball overs were the rule, and until the 1830s all deliveries were underarm. Despite opposition to relaxation of the laws of cricket, overarm delivery was tolerated after 1835, provided that the ball was bowled and not jerked or thrown, and that the hand was never raised above the shoulder. Some bowlers, and Caffyn was one of its greatest exponents, developed a round-arm technique within these requirements. Oldtimers were later to claim this as the purest and most attractive style of bowling; but it was a difficult art. The advent of faster round-arm deliveries required bodily protection. Pads were introduced in 1841, but not before a fast ball from an Etonian bowler had broken a batsman's leg.

Bowlers soon demanded the right to raise their arm above the shoulder, and in 1864 the rules were revised to allow this. However, both underarm and round-arm techniques co-existed with the new overarm. In the Gentlemen versus Players match at Lord's in 1868, E. M. Grace bowled both underarm and round-arm. Bowling in the 1884 Oval Test match, Alfred Lyttleton captured 4 wickets for 19 runs with his slow underarm lobs. Even in the 1890s, Daft considered that any county team would be advised to play an underarm bowler, because well-directed 'lobs' could penetrate the best defence. Cricket still retained something of its village green origins and was comparatively free of mental attitudes which in a later age produced 'leg theory' and ruthless run-makers.[11]

William Caffyn provides a useful index of the extent of the changes in cricket before and after the Aboriginal tour.[12] Caffyn lived in Australia from 1864 to 1871. Upon his return to England, he was struck by the 'great alterations [which] had taken place in the cricket world'. These included the end of the All-England XI and similar commercial teams; the Gentlemen were victorious over the Players; new county clubs had been formed; wicket preparation had improved considerably; rule changes allowed overarm bowling and, in the 1870s, fours were no longer all run.

The difficulties encountered on English playing fields during the 1860s paled to insignificance by comparison with Australian bush cricket in the gold-rush era. That same decade prove equally critical in the development of the Australian game. The first match played by the enthusiastic Colac club in 1853 provides insight into the standards of country cricket:

Rymer, the wheelwright, ––– [made] two bats, we made the stumps ourselves ––– a shoemaker supplied us with a ball (his own handicraft) for 10/–...we ordered a large supply of bottled beer and porter ...A large crowd gathered on a vacant piece of ground...and here we wielded the willow and trundled the leather...at intervals we started the fiddlers to work, dancing on the green being vigorously indulged in by ladies and gentlemen present...corks flew out of bottles as if by magic, contents vanished in double quick time...the results of game [were] not chronicled.

By the time that the English heroes arrived in 1861, cricket proved so popular that there were more than 70 clubs in Victoria and many Victorian and New South Wales pastoral properties maintained their own teams. Victoria selected 22 men for the first match of Stephenson's tour, although he later insisted on limiting the opposition to 18. Even so, as the result satisfied Stephenson of the overwhelming superiority of his team, in all future encounters his men confidently faced 22 colonists. The English success created a profound impression and Australian batsmen imitated their 'forward' style. At the end of the tour, the recently founded Albert Club in Sydney tempted Charles Lawrence to remain behind and accept a permanent coaching position at their Redfern ground. Lawrence therefore became Australia's first professional coach. Two years later William Caffyn, who returned with Parr's team, briefly became coach at the Melbourne Cricket Ground. Both these appointments of top-flight all-rounders were landmarks in cricketing history. For the first time, also, it was realized that careful preparation of the playing area and rolling the pitch paid dividends. A decade earlier, goats and cattle browsed in the outfield of the MCG, while the rough makeshift pitch at Ballarat was quite uneven. Even so, despite positive developments, W. G. Grace encountered indescribable ground conditions on his 1873 tour. A photograph taken of the MCG during an inter-colonial match in 1860 shows the playing area level, but absolutely bare of grass cover. The hot wind blowing at the time must have baked it hard and fast. Unfortunately for the batsmen, the rule of a boundary stroke registering four runs had not been introduced at that time. Playing fields lacked boundaries in the 1860s and all runs had to be made the strenuous way (Plate 3).[13]

This transitional period was the heyday of 'chucking'. Until the arrival of the English touring side, it was usual to deliver the ball underarm, although Victoria's drawcard and captain, T. W. Wills (who learned his cricket at Rugby), could bowl both underarm and round-arm. Altham suggests that Stephenson, a pioneer of the more thoroughgoing over-arm fast bowling, may have demonstrated his skills in Aus-tralia. As Daft rated Stephenson as one of the best coaches in England, his example may have been influential. In any case, Caffyn and Lawrence instructed colonials in round-arm delivery, an art which they had perfected.

Naturally, the adoption of new techniques caused difficul-ties and posed problems which had echoes in recent times. As a contemporary observed, 'the inexperienced colonials found it difficult to tell when a man was bowling and when he was throwing'. There are grounds for believing that Tom Wills was an adept 'chucker', while even the immortal Spof-forth is said to have sometimes thrown the ball. As in England, underarm and round-arm styles were continued for many years; overs consisted of four balls; umpiring was of indifferent quality, and the visiting team normally supplied an umpire. Leather balls were standard in England, but in Australia composition balls were commonly used, except in important matches when leather balls were bowled. When the Aboriginal team visited Rochdale in 1868, Hamlet Nicholson presented each man with a compound ball from his factory. They responded by presenting him with a testimonial 'showing that his cricket balls had been in use in Australia for many years, and are highly appreciated'.[14]

Stephenson's tour proved so successful that no sponsor was needed for the next visit to Australia. In 1863–64 George Parr captained a team of 12 self-financed cricketers which returned home £7000 richer. During each of its 16 matches the team faced twice its number, but even against such odds it won 10 and drew and other six games. An innovation on this tour was the combination of cricket with an athletics meeting in which the players participated. Obviously, with cricket an investment business there was every reason to promote 'brighter cricket'. In England at this period, the Surrey Club stimulated crowd-pleasing cricket by presenting a bat to any player who scored 50 runs at the Oval. It is evident that business ethics fostered action cricket even before the Aboriginal tour.

The term 'athletics' as used in England and Australia at this time covered a multitude of activities. It was a collective term embracing running, jumping, throwing and more. 'Pedestrianism' was another alternative designation referring particularly to running and hurdling. While the term 'games' may have been more appropriate for some of the more unorthodox events, it was not favoured. In the current ethos, athletics or athletic sports were considered terms which more aptly conveyed the stern, serious intent of competition. At a two-day athletics meeting in Manchester in 1867, in addition to races and jumps, competitors fenced, boxed and wrestled, putt the shot and threw the cricket ball, among other events. The following year, the Aborigines were to add even greater variety to an English athletics meeting.[15]

Athletic events became customary in the Australian colonies. An amateur athletics sports club was formed in 1864 as part of the Melbourne Cricket Club. When the Duke of Edinburgh visited Melbourne in 1867, the cricket match held in his honour at the MCG ended with a sports meeting. It was on this same day that a grand, free banquet was staged in the zoological gardens. A crowd of 100,000 citizens seeking a place with royalty surged forward, frightened the Duke away, scoffed the food and broached the 500-gallon wine cask which supplied the fountain erected as centrepiece for the banquet. Colonial society was raucous and brash; the practices of cricket had to fall in with such requirements, even if the rules apparently remained inflexible.[16]

When Caffyn returned to Australia with Parr's team, he remained until 1871, coaching at the MCG for a year before moving to Sydney, where he combined coaching duties at the Warwick club with a hairdressing business in George Street. Caffyn had a striking influence on Victorian cricket during his brief stay, while in Sydney, he and Lawrence were responsible for a marked increase in the standard of play.

Both men were all-rounders of merit and proved efficient teachers. T. W. Wills was the third vital figure in raising the quality of colonial cricket. Born in 1835, he was sent to Rugby by his Victorian pastoralist father in 1852, where he captained the school team in cricket and football and proved a successful round-arm bowler. Later he played for Cambridge (for which university he enrolled but never entered), and also in Ireland. He returned to become secretary of the Melbourne Cricket Club in 1857. Wills acted as coach to various teams during his career and took 80 wickets for Victoria, but his immortality in Melbourne sporting circles rests with another game. He was one of the founders (or inventors) of Australian Rules football, which every winter packs the MCG with as many people as once attempted to gatecrash the ducal banquet at the zoo. It was Wills who gave the Aboriginal cricketers their first professional coaching; Lawrence captained them on their English tour.[17]

Despite the advent of professionals, Australian play by the end of the decade was undistinguished. When that champion of amateurism, W. G. Grace, was induced (at a personal profit of £1500) to captain the third All-England XI in 1873, his men (who received only £70 each) were opposed by teams of 18 players. They even defeated a combined Victorian–New South Wales XVIII, although they were beaten by a Victorian team, the first local victory against England on the Melbourne Cricket Ground. The 1881–82 tourists played 18 of their 25 fixtures against odds, while even Lord Sheffield's 1891–92 touring team faced superior numbers in 19 of 27 matches. Whether or not the explanation for low scoring lay with poor wicket conditions or mediocre batting technique, the fact remains that, prior to 1879, only two centuries had been scored in intercolonial contests. Whenever thoughts of nostalgic commentators stray to the Victorian era as a golden age of cricket, it is worth recalling such realities.[18]

While attendance figures indicate sustained support for cricket during the nineteenth century, Europeans were not alone in their enthusiasm for the game. This period witnessed an interesting cricketing phenomenon in the widespread participation of Aborigines. Matches beween different Victorian Aboriginal missions and settlements were frequent, and many Aborigines also played in New South Wales. Perhaps the most startling example of Aboriginal prowess is contained in the enigmatic news item in the *Sydney Morning Herald* (6 February 1869) concerning young Johnny Taylor, a member of the Ginninderra team, an area now within the Australian Capital Territory, who scored '35 runs for 4 hits'.

The publication of Samuel Shumack's reminiscences of Canberra provides background to his feat. Johnny's father was also a competent cricketer, but young Johnny eclipsed European and Aboriginal players alike in the Ginninderra team. His record stroke (presumably upon the occasion cited above) was a hit from which he scored 10 runs. He was a natural big hitter, and on another occasion he was reported to have struck a ball which carried for 165 yards before touching ground. During the early 1860s, three Aborigines played in the locally victorious Ginninderra team, although Aboriginal membership dates from at least 1856. Only one case of discrimination against their membership is known, when in 1861 a Duntroon club member refused to play against them. As they continued to play in the team until death removed Johnny's father and Johnny departed for employment as head stockman and horsebreaker on a station near Tumut, it is evident that prejudices were outweighed by tolerance. Like so many of his race, his father included, Johnny died prematurely from measles in 1875.[19]

Cricket was popular also in the Riverina by 1862. A correspondent along the Lachlan River reported lively Aboriginal players near Deniliquin, where 'Booligal Jacky' and four of his mates had challenged five Europeans to a match. In the same year, *The Victorian Cricketer's Guide,* possibly drawing upon this item, remarked favourably upon the introduction of cricket 'among the native blacks on the Murray, who have become no mean proficients [*sic*] in the game, especially at fielding'.[20]

An even earlier occurrence of Aboriginal cricket may be inferred in South Australia, although in this instance it concerned the missionary institution of Poonindie, near Port Lincoln. An 1854 painting of a Poonindie Aboriginal cricketer by John Michael Crossland is in the National Library of Australia (Plate 5). The future Bishop M. B. Hale became founding superintendent of Poonindie Anglican Mission in 1850. He soon realized that cricket possessed therapeutic value within Aboriginal society. In his chronicle of the mission, Bishop Hale discussed the problems of instilling sedentary habits into his charges and of so controlling and 'civilizing' them into European ways. They suffered from frequent moods of depression and 'became ill and restless; they long for change of scene, and thus are tempted to stray back into the Bush. Cricketing, therefore, was introduced with great success'. This portrait of young Nannultera is among the earliest pictorial evidence for Aboriginal cricketers. A photograph taken in the 1870s of Aboriginal cricketers, at Point Macleay mission, demonstrates that the game's popularity had spread among the Aboriginal community in South Australia (Plates 6 & 7). By 1864, the Victorian Board for the Protection of the Aborigines boasted that 'good old English songs' and cricket were popular at some Aboriginal welfare stations.[21]

More detailed evidence from Victoria is provided by H. N. Moseley, a naturalist aboard HMS *Challenger* during its scientific expedition. Late in March 1874 Moseley visited the Coranderrk Aboriginal station near Healesville. He reported: 'we found the cricket party in high spirits, shouting with laughter, rows of spectators being seated on logs and chaffing the players with old English sallies: "well hit"; "run it out"; "butter fingers"...the men were all dressed as Europeans; they knew all about Mr W. G. Grace and the All-England Eleven.'

Moseley wanted to procure a platypus, for they abounded in the creek which ran through the settlement. To his annoyance, although he offered seven shillings and sixpence for a dead specimen, five shillings above the usual price, 'no one thought of leaving the cricket or his looking on at the game; nor, though I offered a good price for a boomerang, did any one care to fetch one from the village'.[22] Fortunately, this cricket field was photographed a few years after Moseley's visit. It shows a row of spectators and at least 14 hirsute fieldsmen (Plate 8).

Later in the century, Aboriginal enthusiasm for cricket was encouraged at mission settlements in southern Queensland, and the Deebing Creek team from near Ipswich met with success during the 1890s (Plate 9). An Aboriginal, Albert Henry, was included sporadically in the Queensland

State team between 1901 and 1905.[23] The most celebrated team from this period, however, played in Western Australia. Bishop R. Salvado, the venerable Benedictine Abbot of New Norcia, in 1879 encouraged H. B. Lefroy, a local European pastoralist, to form an Aboriginal cricket team. After a period of coaching, they played a number of matches. During this time they were photographed in their trim uniform of blue dungaree trousers, blue striped white woollen shirts and blue, rimless, band-box cap tied with a tape under the chin. Two blue ribbons encircled the cap, while a narrow brighter blue ribbon placed centrally over the other ribbons added a touch of distinction (Plates 10 & 11). They walked to matches in Perth and Fremantle.

Unfortunately, nervousness cost them victory on the occasion of their first appearance on the Perth ground. A subsequent series of wins soon converted them into the Invincibles, their club name until its disbandonment in 1906. When Sydney's Cardinal Moran visited New Norcia in 1887, the team played the local Europeans. They scored 160 runs in their innings and then twice dismissed their opponents for a total of 47 runs. They won a trophy at Toodyay in 1881, inscribed 'to the New Norcia Aboriginal cricket team for their prowess in the field'.

Evidently, Salvado sought in cricket a means of substituting this new form of group ritual activity for traditional ceremonial life, whose abandonment he encouraged. An observer of a victory in 1879 described captain Alec Wenola being carried off the field on the shoulders of his enthusiastic team. According to Daisy Bates 'the bishop had observed the absorption of the young natives in the game... played by the white settlers'. She also remarked that one reason for their success at the game was their agility and quickness of eye. Indeed, this may help to explain the apparent decline in cricket's popularity with Aborigines after the turn of the century.

The cricketers referred to in all these accounts were normally persons of full Aboriginal descent, a fact emphasized by Bates about the New Norcia men. They also were relatively young. Even at Coranderrk, fewer than 80 kilometres from Melbourne, hunting activities were practised commonly and, despite strenuous attempts by missionaries or superintendents to suppress them, ceremonial rites almost certainly continued in the bush at discreet distances from settlements. They definitely took place at New Norcia around 1880. Salvado recorded a major ceremonial gathering some 80 kilometres distant involving the display of sacred ritual objects. An estimated 300 people arrived from the north, having travelled considerable distances; other groups came from the east to join them. Despite the efforts of missionaries to suppress traditional ritual life, it is evident that it still supplied cohesion and motivation in the face of European pressure.[24]

The communal team organization and its concomitant barracking, remarked upon by Moseley, possibly provided a partial 'ritual' substitute for people under stress. From a sociological perspective, sport should not be assessed only for its primarily physical aspects, but also for the social–psychological interaction involved. It might be considered that, if sport is the safety-valve of the people, especially the urban masses, possibly it served a similar cathartic function in racial contact situations. Besides, cricket was a sport which gave a bonus for the qualities possessed by keen-sighted huntsmen, and which placed the Aborigines in a unique position of advantage in relation to Europeans. It seems possible, also, that the evident success of Aborigines in mastering an English sport won grudging admiration from those Europeans, whose opinion of Aboriginal achievement was otherwise poor. Daisy Bates observed that 'wherever the team went it was treated as a body of sportsmen and gentlemen', and this response is discussed later. Later in the century as tribal cohesion and economic organization weakened, as new generations grew to manhood in a European-dominated society, and as the original players aged, both the appeal and the inherent advantages of cricket diminished. The rise of Western District cricket, and its climax in the 1868 English tour, is best considered in the light of these developments. It is likely, however, that a further ingredient promoting Aboriginal cricket involvement during the closing decades of the century was the fame of these Victorian cricketers among Aboriginal communities.[25]

In 1863, William Westgarth surveyed the history and social institutions of Victoria and included cricket among them. He praised colonial efforts to challenge the All-English XI and added a timely, yet prophetic note:[26]

> There is yet another rival party coming upon the horizon, which may some of these days furnish its formidable elevens. The Aboriginal natives have entered with ardour into cricket. The Aborigines of the Lachlan are already players. They are described as sure at the bat and capital at blocking, with their keen eyesight.

NOTES

[1] The events of the 1861–62 tour are based upon K. Dunstan, *The Paddock That Grew* (Melbourne, 1962), 26; H. S. Altham, *A History of Cricket* (London, 1962), vol 1, 131; W. Caffyn, *Seventy-one Not Out* (London, 1899), 171, 202; C. Lawrence, MS 1, 49–52.

[2] The views of Grace are presented in the second chapter of his '*W. G.*' *Cricketing Reminiscences* (London, 1899).

[3] Details about professional cricket come chiefly from W. F. Mandle, 'The professional cricketer in England in the nineteeth century', *Labour History*, no 23 (1972):1–16; ('money-grabbing', p 9), and H. Cunningham, *Leisure in the Industrial Revolution c 1780–c 1880* (New York, 1980), 113. R. Daft, *Kings of Cricket* (Bristol, 1893), records a number of simple pranks.

[4] For Trollope, see his preface to his *British Sports and Pastimes* (London, 1868).

[5] Trollope, *British Sports*, 307–10.

[6] Player's strike: Mandle 11.

[7] Wellington, Waterloo and 'Drake': Lord W. Lennox, *Pictures of Sporting Life and Character*, 2 vols (London, 1860), vol 2, 180, 183.

[8] Triumph of Gentlemen: Mandle, 2; Cunningham, *Leisure*, 113; B. Haley, *The Healthy Body and Victorian Culture* (Harvard, 1978), 125.

[9] Treloar's 'circus', Mandle, 10.

[10] Ground conditions are described by Grace, *Reminiscences*, esp. Ch 2 and in his *The History of a Hundred Centuries* (London, 1895), 14; Daft, *Kings of Cricket*, 206; Altham, *History*, ch 10; P. F. Warner, *Lord's 1787–1945* (London, 1946); Lawrence, MS 1, 20; Turnham Green is mentioned in *Cricket Scores and Biographies*, vol 10, 659. Death at the wicket: E. Parker, *The History of Cricket* (London, n.d.), 141.

[11] The changing rules are described by C. Box, *The English Game of Cricket* (London, 1877), ch 24; Daft, *Kings*, 236; Altham, *History*, 63, 121; F. Gale, *Modern English Sports* (London, 1885), 21–2 (pads); Lyttleton: Huge Field, personal communication.

[12] W. Caffyn, *Seventy-one Not Out* (London, 1899), 228–31.

[13] The Colac match description is provided in Isaac Hebb, *History of Colac and District* (Melbourne, 1970), 351. Australian ground conditions are described by C. P. Moody, *Australian Cricket and Cricketers* (Melbourne, 1894), 3; Grace, *Reminiscences*, 104; W. F. Mandle, 'Cricket and Australian nationalism in the nineteenth century', *Journal of the Royal Historical Society*, 59 (1973), 227.

[14] 'Chucking' is inferred from Altham, *History*, 99; Daft, *Kings*, 76; Moody, *Australian Cricket*, 4, 43. Nicholson balls: *Roch. Obs.*, 11 July 1868.

[15] The term 'athletics' is dicussed by Haley, *The Healthy Body*, 131, 137. The Surrey bat: Grace, *Reminiscences*, 19. Caffyn, *Seventy-one*, 203, 209, refers to athletic contests on the 1864 tour.

[16] The zoo party: *Argus* (Melbourne), 29 November 1867; J. Milner and O. W. Brierly, *The Cruise of H. M. S. Galatea* (London, 1869), 245–8.

[17] Wills is discussed by A. G. Moyes, *Australian Cricket: A History* (Sydney, 1959), 113. His role in developing Australian Rules football is examined by Ian Turner, *Up There Cazaly* (Melbourne, 1979). On this theme, also see W. F. Mandle, 'Games people played: cricket and football in England and Victoria in the late nineteenth century', *Historical Studies*, 15 (1973), 520.

[18] The quality of colonial cricket is inferred from F. J. Ironside, *50 Years of Cricket* (Sydney, 1895); Moody, *Australian Cricket*, and H.

Heaton, *Australian Dictionary of Dates and Men of the Time* (Sydney, 1879), part 2, 79.

[19] Ginninderra cricketers: S. Shumack, *Tales and Legends of Canberra Pioneers* (Canberra, 1967), 150; E. Lea-Scarlett, *Queanbeyan District and People* (Queanbeyan, 1968), 130–1; L. Gillespie, *Canberra Times*, 16 January 1982, 15.

[20] Lachlan cricket: *The Illustrated Melbourne Post*, 20 September 1862; Murray cricket: W. J. Hammersley, *The Victorian Cricketer's Guide* (Melbourne, 1862), 164.

[21] The description of Poonindie cricket comes from M. B. Hale, *The Aborigines of Australia* (London, 1889), 97. The Crossland painting is discussed by John Tregenza, 'Two notable portraits of South Australian Aborigines', *Journal of the Historical Soc. of S. Aust.* No 12 (1984), 22–31. English songs and cricket: *Fourth report, Board for the Protection of Aborigines*, 1864, 9.

[22] H. N. Moseley, *Notes by a Naturalist* (London, 1879), 262. When Moseley returned to England he taught Zoology at Oxford and became a significant influence upon the career of Baldwin Spencer, whose later work with Aborigines proved so important.

[23] Queensland developments have been traced by Genevieve Blades, in an unpublished thesis, 'Australian Aborigines, Cricket and Pedestrianism: Culture and Conflict 1880–1910', University of Queensland, 1985.

[24] The significance of New Norcia cricket was first described by D. M. Bates, 'An Aboriginal cricket team', *Aust.*, 12 January 1924, 94, and 26 February 1927, 524. There is a brief account and photograph in Lois Tilbrook, *Nyungar Tradition* (Perth, 1983), 199. References to Bishop Salvado have been supplied from his diaries by courtesy of the librarian of the Benedictine Abbey of the Holy Trinity, New Norcia. Identification of the team and the Toodyay trophy comes from G. Russo, *Lord Abbot of the Wilderness* (Melbourne, 1980), 243–4, 264.

[25] For the role of sport in modern society, see D. W. Ball and J. W. Loy, *Sport and Social Order* (Reading, 1975).

[26] The cricketing prophecy was by William Westall, *The Colony of Victoria: Its History, Commerce and Gold Mining; Its Social and Political Institutions Down to the End of 1863* (London, 1864), 449.

2

Black Cricketers

The country in the Harrow–Edenhope area of western Victoria was taken up for pastoral occupation around 1844–46, although detailed references to it by contemporaries are scant. Twenty years later, the local Aborigines were playing cricket with the pastoral pioneers. An idyllic situation, perhaps, indicative of tolerance and enlightened racial attitudes. It was not always so harmonious (Figure A).

When the settlers arrived with their flocks this was good country, for the most part well watered and grassed, with the capacity to maintain a considerable Aboriginal population. When the Hamilton family settled at Bringalbert, north of Apsley, the country was lightly timbered with red and white gum and she-oak; excellent summer feed, long kangaroo-grass, covered the spaces between the trees. After a few years of stocking with hard-hoofed, close-cropping domestic animals, which compacted the soil and scuffed the edible root stock, the face of the earth changed. Native grasses had evolved to nourish animals with different feeding habits. Indiscriminate firing by settlers also played a part in fostering the growth of worthless scrub across former pastures, while the summer-growing kangaroo-grass was replaced under grazing by introduced winter-growing grasses and weeds.

The land was rich also in native fauna. Indeed, the settlers found it too well stocked in the 1860s, perhaps resulting from the concentration of animals in less-settled areas. The *Hamilton Spectator* claimed that 150,000 kangaroos were slaughtered on two stations in the Warrnambool area within a few years. At the conclusion of a single day's organized drive on another station in 1867, 6000 dead kangaroos were counted and another 2000 were killed two months later.

However, the Aboriginal inhabitants had not depended upon hunting alone, for this country was exceptionally rich in terms of a hunter-gatherer economy. Recent research has demonstrated that nutritious and abundant plant foods were available to sustain populations through the annual cycle. The staple plant was the daisy yam (*Microseris scapigera*), known as *murnong* or by some other Aboriginal variant by early settlers who saw Aborigines roasting the tubers or corms in the ashes. The many swamps, lakes and creeks provided further tuberous roots rich in carbohydrate, including bulrush (*Typha* spp.) and ribbonweed (*Triglochin procera*), while numerous species of ground orchids were eaten. Other roots which are high in fibre were pounded to extract the starch, particularly bracken (*Pteridium esculatum*). Where the incoming settlers faced starvation in what they conceived of as wilderness, Aboriginal inhabitants manipulated a bountiful harvest. The murnong was so plentiful and nutritious that it would have been possible, though rather monotonous, to have lived on it virtually alone.[1]

Archaeologists have recovered evidence for the systematic exploitation of lake and swamp resources, either through the use of stone fish traps or woven plant weirs and baskets. The most elaborate system known was at Lake Condah, where different sets of stone fish traps came into operaton at each major fluctuation in water level. The most remarkable 'discovery', resulting from the careful re-evaluation of written records in conjunction with field survey, concerns eel fishing. Eels were harvested on a vast scale in the Western District and the manner in which it was attempted merit the term 'manipulation', if not 'farming'. One of the most important sites is at Toolondo, in the heartland of the Aboriginal team which is the subject of this book. In a complex of artificial channels which once connected swamps, including two systems separated by a rise, a total length of 3.75 kilometres was dug (Plate 12). Some sections are narrow drains, but almost a kilometre consisted of a drain more than two metres wide and a metre deep. They were evidently dug and maintained using wooden shovels. A radiocarbon sample has been obtained for what is interpreted as a late stage of infilling in the drain's operation. It is 210 ± 120 years before the present. While not a precise date, this suggests that it was a pre-European construction; although the date of its origin is unknown. A comparable eel fishery was seen in operation during 1841, on Mt William station. From a creek ran a maze of artificial channels which covered more than 3.5 hectares, providing opportunities for trapping the eels in the channels. With surplus food supplies available regionally, Aborigininal society was characterized by ceremonial gatherings of several hundred people at appropriate times. This would have represented more people than those attending a Western District agricultural and pastoral show or sporting event during the first decades of European control.[2]

Prior to these discoveries, the Aboriginal population of western Victoria was assumed to be relatively small, but it now seems reasonable to postulate a greater population density. Along the southern coast, where varied and plentiful food supplies existed, one person could have been sustained by the resources of two to three square kilometres. In the inland, resources may have been less abundant, although the swamps with their varied food supplies, including the manipulation of eels, must have sustained a higher population than hitherto credited. There is literary and archaeological evidence for the existence of semi-permanent settlements in the region. Around Mt William, it has been estimated that population density may have ranged between 2.6 and 3.9 square kilometres per person. The same calculations assign almost 8000 people to the Western District, instead of the 3000–4000 usually claimed.

The Aboriginal cricketers belonged chiefly to two main

divisions, which Europeans, following American and African practice, called tribes. Most of them were Madimadi (Marditjali in N. B. Tindale's tribal nomenclature), whose area centred upon Lake Wallace, site of the future Edenhope. Further north was the drier mallee scrub country, where the Wutjubaluk (Wotjbaluk) people ranged over a wider tract of Wimmera and southern Mallee districts. Using a thumb as a calculator, and given that the cricketers originated within the area enclosed by lines connecting modern Hamilton, Casterton, Naracoorte, Kaniva and Horsham back to Hamilton, the estimates described above are reduced to an average density of one person per five square kilometres, the population of the region at the instant of European contact may have numbered 2000 persons or more.

In 1863, the Board for Protection of Aborigines attempted a population census in Victoria. The same area as that designated above was believed to contain fewer than 300 Aborigines. Yet Hamilton believed that when he arrived at Bringalbert, on the fringes of the drier country and some years after the initial European settlement, there were 300 Aborigines within a radius of only 80 kilometres of the station. These estimates are tentative, but the proportions are suggestive of decimation of the original inhabitants.[3]

It is significant that when the manager of the Aboriginal cricket team was recruiting some additional members early in 1867, he found that his choice was limited. His players were 'literally the last of their tribe, those left up country being merely a few old men and lubras'. As early as 1858 an *Age* editorial (28 October) predicated the extinction of Victoria's Aborigines. In commending humanitarian activities, it coined a catchphrase, exhorting readers to 'smooth the pillow of a dying race'. Official attitudes were revealed starkly in the *Handbook of Victoria for the Colonial and Indian Exhibition*, staged in London in 1886. 'The existence of the few (Aborigines) that still remain alive has no political or social significance whatever. The race will probably become extinct in the course of a few years.'[4]

The harsh reality, therefore, is that in this rapidly depopulating region of western Victoria, European tolerance may have stemmed from feelings of security and indifference. Peope of mixed race were either ignored or treated as 'poor whites'. Settlers were certain that their rights to the land would go unchallenged by the ageing and diseased survivors from its prehistoric occupation. A mood of sentimental romanticism, even a nostalgia for times past, pervades some paintings of this era. *Minjah in the old time* is such an example of serenity which contrasted so dramatically with reality (Plate 16A). A few years after this idyllic scene was painted, the Aboriginal team crossed Minjah lands on its trek to Geelong.

Such sentiments were not shared by those pastoral pioneers who moved into the area during the 1840s, droving their flocks from further south or east, where most of them had settled initially. The experience of squatters from the lower Glenelg area, in particular, had embittered them towards the Aborigines, for the original land occupants resisted the land takers. As an example of their hazardous occupation, settlers in the Port Fairy pastoral district claimed in a petition in 1841 that, during a two-month period, they suffered the following losses: four Europeans killed and six wounded; 3700 sheep stolen or maimed (although most were recovered); horses and cattle speared; arson and robbery of dwellings. There is little doubt that the situation during the early 1840s in this region was more difficult than that in most Victorian areas. While settlers may have exaggerated their difficulties in order to ensure government action, this region was densely occupied, so resistance was understandable. Settler retaliation, assisted by H. P. Dana and his central Victorian native police force, was drastic. It is probable that numerous indiscriminate killings took place. P. L. S. Chauncey, an intelligent visitor to the same area in 1848, commented that 'the natives are very few in number and quite peaceable. Those who were not shot by the first settlers have almost all died off with a loathsome disease'. Passing tourists could afford to be frank in their diaries; with a governor who claimed to be concerned for Aboriginal welfare, settlers were more circumspect. As the informative *Letters from Victorian Pioneers* to Governor La Trobe exemplify, settlers either denied such actions or blamed uncouth neighbours.[5]

A recent evaluation of the documentary evidence for the number of Aboriginal and settler murders in Victoria before 1850 concluded that a minimum of 400 Aborigines met violent deaths compared with 59 colonists killed through Aboriginal action. While every European death was reported rapidly in order to ensure swift reprisals, many Aboriginal deaths were not reported, so the number killed is a rough estimate. Few settlers were precise and even the police preferred vague statements in describing their retaliation. Indiscrimate massacres frequently included women and children, thereby causing a rapid decline in the next generation. Of those violent deaths recorded, it is estimated that 159 lives of Western District people were lost. Even this minimal two or three per cent mortality rate in about a decade was low compared with the decimation resulting from European diseases. Even before the first flocks arrived, it is possible that smallpox ravaged the population. Other infectious diseases, especially measles, chest ailments and venereal disease, found receptive hosts among the now displaced, disoriented and poorly nourished Aboriginal population.[6]

The callous indifference of many settlers to Aboriginal lives or conditions is evident in many sources. Two contemporary examples from the Wimmera region illustrate the situation. The first concerns Horatio Spencer Wills, father of the sportsman T. W. Wills. Wills claimed to have established friendly relations with Aborigines near Mt William, where he settled around 1840. This certainly appears to have been the case. On the other hand, when it was proposed, in 1842, to establish an Aboriginal Protectorate station on good land adjacent to his run, his protested to Lieutenant-

Governor La Trobe in a manner which revealed stark self-interest and prejudice which was the norm for even bene-volent settlers. More brutal, however, was the action of a shepherd in the same region.[7] As described by a neighbour of Wills, this shepherd, whom he met while riding across the country, 'held a carbine in the place of a crook, and an old regulation pistol was stuck in his belt, instead of the more classic pastoral pipe. . . After some conversation he led me to a waterhole, where the skeleton of a native — exposed by the shrinking of the water in the summer heat — lay on the mud. There was a bullet-hole through the back of the skull. "He was shot in the water," the man told me, "as he was a-trying to hid hisself after a scrimmage! There was a lot more tother side. . . I might see the bones a-sticking up out of the ground close to the big fallen gum-tree, where they'd been stowed away all of a heap" — a grave good enough, he. . .assure(d) me, for the "sneaking, murdering, black cannibal"'.

Race relations further west took a similar course. When W. Brown was murdered near Lake Wallace in July 1845 squatter reaction was immediate. J. C. Hamilton, whose brother 20 years later was to initiate the Aborigines on his station into the mysteries of cricket, recorded approvingly events which preceded his family's arrival in the area.[8] There must have been similar episodes, carefully kept from public notice:

It was necessary to teach the blacks a lesson, and the station people met and decided to take the law into their own hands. . .a call to arms was made. . .It was a bad day for the ill-fated darkies. The horsemen came up with them in the ranges behind Narracoorte, and saw one fellow carrying poor Brown's gun, and a lubra wearing a coat. They made no show of resistance. . .The lesson given to the blacks that day made them understand they must respect the lives of white men.

By 1864 available land in western Victoria had been selected for pastoral occupation and small settlements developed along the bush tracks between stations. Roads of importance radiated from Hamilton, the regional centre, while the road to South Australia through Naracoorte was an important route in gold-rush days. Harrow, nestling on the steep slopes of the Glenelg Valley, was one of these rural centres. Apsley, a hamlet on the Naracoorte road nearer the border, was another. In addition to a church and graveyard, a single store and its popular inn, Apsley boasted a racing club and it was the local centre for the annual Pastoral and Agricultural Society show. Between these two rude settlements lay the future Edenhope, on the shores of Lake Wallace. It was destined to outstrip its rivals; even then it supported two stores and three bush inns. Mounted Constable Kennedy led a busy life and his lock-up was in demand, for the thirst of Edenhope district's 120 European inhabitants was notorious even in Hamilton, more than 100 kilometres away. There was another lock-up conveniently available in Harrow. Constructed in 1859 of rough logs placed horizontally, it stands solidly there today, while most of the township has decayed (Plate 16).

In August 1864 the area became renowned throughout the colony, and eventually the Empire, for one of the acts of heroism so dear to sentimental Victorian hearts. Three children became lost in the bush on the eastern fringes of the Little Desert. The saga of Jane, Isaac and Frank Duff who wandered from Spring Hill station, north of Apsley and Harrow, was told in the national press, and it was retold to generations of school children through the moralizing story in the Education Department of Victoria's Grade Four reader. Three Aboriginal trackers were brought from Mt Elgin station further north, near modern Nhill, and on the ninth day they found the children alive. Isaac and Frank had been sustained by seven-year-old Jane, despite rain, frost and lack of food.

An emotional public subscribed generously to a fund for Jane, wrote verses and erected monuments in her honour. The Aborigines who found her were rewarded with £20, £5 of which they proceeded to spend at the nearest pub. Most sources fail to mention their names; those which do agree that 'King Richard' or Dick-a-Dick was one of them, but give various names for the others, including Red Cap. Dick-a-Dick and Red Cap toured England with the 1868 cricket team, although at that time Dick-a-Dick was a model of sobriety.

Edenhope acquired a cricket club around this period. With the All-England XI tours stimulating bush imitators, no settlement seemed too remote to field a team. William Reginald Hayman (1842–99) was the driving force in promoting Edenhope's club. His uncle, J. P. Hayman, emigrated from Devon and had settled on Lake Wallace South station in 1855; as a Justice of the Peace, he was a prominent citizen. It is interesting that Peter, an Aboriginal from the Hayman property, represented the club in its first fixture. Balmoral, situated further south on the Hamilton road, fielded a cricket team also, and the massive Bullocky was a member. These two foundation members of European clubs joined the team which toured England.[9]

In 1864, also, the youthful and athletic Thomas Gibson Hamilton of Bringalbert station began teaching the rudiments of cricket to Aborigines in his employ, an interest shared with William Hayman. It was fortunate that the latest cricketing techniques, including round-arm bowling, were communicated by a schoolboy home from Melbourne's Scotch College. He was James T. Edgar, the son of David Edgar, who occupied Pine Hill station between Edenhope and Harrow in 1855. Further assistance came from Edgar's neighbour and former partner, John Bryan Fitzgerald (1821–71), who had moved recently from Portland to Mullagh station. Fitzgerald had been an active sportsman in Portland, including a period on the committee of the Portland cricket club. The simple vernacular single-storey homestead on Mullagh, named after an Irish locality, was still under construction at this time. Like Pine Hill homestead, the original section of which dates from around 1858, Mullagh homestead survives as a memorial to the cricket initiative with which they were associated. The most distinguished Aboriginal cricketer of his generation would be Johnny Mullagh. Originally known as Black Johnny, he was a groom on Pine Hill, until he moved to work for Fitzgerald on Mullagh station. He passed most of his life on these two properties, whose combined area exceeded 40,000 hectares and probably included his clan territory. Johnny Mullagh, as he had become by 1865, practised his game on a level stretch of hard ground near Mullagh homstead.[10]

Some 40 kilometres north-east, near the eel harvesting channels at Toolondo, cricket evidently prospered on Mount Talbot station. Charles Myles Officer (1827–1904) was captain of the Upper Glenelg cricket club, a team which challenged the Aboriginal team at Balmoral during March 1866. Officer was sufficiently interested in Aboriginal society to learn the local language and, later in life, to become a member of the Central Board for the Protection of the Aborigines. With 15,000 sheep on some of the best Merino pastures in the colony, he employed a number of Aboriginal seasonal workers. He set an example by paying them the same wages as his European hands received. The station day-books for the years 1864–66 contain the names of at least five Aborigines which are identical to those of cricketers in the first regular Aboriginal team.

Although there is no direct evidence for Aborigines playing at Mount Talbot, a late-nineteenth-century photograph shows a match in progress between Europeans adjacent to the attractive two-storey homestead which was completed in 1866 (Plates 13–15). Circumstantial evidence suggests that Aborigines were coached there. A contemporary stated that Bullocky was taught by C. M. Officer, and Bullocky's name appears on the 1864 payroll. Billy Officer proved a less proficient player, but his name is suggestive of a connection. There also was Harry Rose, whose photograph was taken in the 1860s by the proudly proprietorial station management. He stands beside the cup which the Balmoral pastoral society awarded to Mount Talbot in 1864 for exhibiting the prize imported Merino ram; presumably Rose was the prize Aboriginal (Plate 30). It may be inferred that other cricketing stars employed there during this period were Sugar, Neddy (Jim Crow), and Stock-keeper.[11]

It is evident that cricketing conditions for a number of these teams were rudimentary, but details are few. Cuzens may be taken as a typical Aboriginal recruit. He developed into a fine all-rounder, but he learned to bat with a hurdle bar in those Arcadian days. Like the vexed question of whether Batman or Fawkner founded Melbourne, priority in this coaching venture is disputed, and confirmation is lacking in the sources. Initially, it appears a thoroughly co-operative and selfless venture by several enterprising young men, so that credit should be shared. Most of those involved were probably about the same age as the Aborigines whom they instructed. With the country tamed and the tide of pastoral prosperity flowing, cricket must have provided an outlet for a generation with some leisure time. Hayman was later described as a popular amateur entertainer, 'his forte being comic songs in character'. It seems possible, also, that some of the financial support which assisted the team during its early seasons may have come from original land-takers with a guilty conscience.

Initially, however, the most forceful character involved was Tom Hamilton, who provided the drive. A zestful athlete and horseman, he had much in common with his Mount Gambier contemporary, the restless poet Adam Lindsay Gordon. Both of them raced at the Apsley track, and both met premature deaths. J. C. Hamilton reported that the Aborigines 'loved him like a brother', and that he promoted their interests. A letter which Tom later wrote in Hayman's defence, against claims that he exploited the Aboriginal team members, proves him to be a loyal comrade and no seeker of praise: the embodiment of the concept of bush mateship. The lure of adventure and greener pastures led Hamilton to drove horses across Australia in 1872. Following the new overland telegraph route through the MacDonnell Ranges and on to Darwin, he sold his travelled animals for little profit at the end of a 3000-kilometre walk. He died of malaria in Queensland a year later, at 29 years of age.[12]

During 1865 station cricket became so popular that a match was arranged between Europeans and Aborigines representing several stations. It was played on rough ground near the Bringalbert woolshed and the Aborigines were victorious. The following stations were among those involved in the match; known individual participants are included in brackets. Benayeo (D. McLeod and W. O. Groom), Bringalbert (T. Hamilton), Brippick (A. A. Cowell), Hynam (T. Smith), Lake Wallace South (W. R. Hayman), Mortat, also known as Rose Banks (W. Douglas). Pine Hill (David Edgar) and Mullagh (J. C. Fitzgerald) presumably participated, while other possible affiliates were Mount Talbot, Miga Lake, Fulham and Struan. All were properties in the area, mostly in the Edenhope–Harrow region.[13]

The Bringalbert result apparently encouraged Hamilton and Hayman to bring some of the Aborigines to Edenhope, where they practised with the local team every Saturday. They camped and practised on the foreshore of Lake Wallace, near today's high school. On the first occasion when the Aborigines challenged the Edenhope club, they were defeated. However, in the interim before the return game, they mastered the art of round-arm bowling and won by an innings. The game was played on 24 January 1866, again at Bringalbert: Edenhope club scored 36 and 26, while the Aborigines made 75, thereby winning by an innings and 13 runs. Until this match, they had only bowled underarm. As the future bowling star Mullagh was taught round-arm delivery by Edgar, it is possible that he was responsible for this general innovation. It is relevant that Edgar's Scotch College schooldays spanned the exciting times of the first and second All-England XI tours, with their stimulus to cricketing practice. Experience had welded the Aborigines into a combination superior to the social Edenhope club which sponsored them. It was time to match them against better opposition.

This last victory at Bringalbert had made the Aboriginal team newsworthy, and the *Hamilton Spectator* commented approvingly upon their achievement, and added that they might challenge the Hamilton club. When the game did take place in March 1866, the paper described it at length. Tom Hamilton captained the team and, according to his brother, bore the costs of transport. Hayman accompanied them. The team's appearance made a great impression on the partisan crowd which supported its every move. Dressed alike in white trousers, shirts with red trimming, red belts and straw hats with blue band, Hamilton's men were neat, well-spoken, and 'certainly show to better advantage than any Aboriginals we have ever seen'.

The Aboriginal team scored 64 and 52, easily outclassing Hamilton's 36 and 30. Mullagh's five wickets in the second innings were obtained with round-arm deliveries, 'very moderate pace, but a good pitch and a strong twist'. He also starred in the sports meeting which followed. He cleared the bar with a jump of 5 feet 3 inches and threw a cricket ball 110 yards. The newspaper anticipated many later assessments of Mullagh's talent when it rated his performance as 'astonishingly effective'. Following contemporary convention, the visitors were given first use of the wicket. Evidently, however, that was the limit to the sporting sentiments of the home side. When a 'capital' dinner was provided for the visitors at the Criterion Hotel, hosted by the mayor, only two of the Hamilton cricketers attended. These were the captain and James Donaldson, a member of the Cavendish club, included in the Hamilton team because of his superior abilities on the field. The team's absence 'was much commented upon', the *Hamilton Spectator* noted adversely. Six of these victorious Aborigines were to tour England within two years — Mullagh, Cuzens, Bullocky, Peter, Sundown and Neddy (later known as Jim Crow). Of the remainder, Tarpot was selected to travel, but withdrew. Jellico and Sugar died before that time, while Billy Officer travelled to Sydney with the team.

On their return journey to Edenhope, a challenge match was arranged at Balmoral against the Upper Glenelg club, captained by Charles Officer. The ubiquitous Donaldson played for yet another team and Mullagh again attracted notice by scoring 31 runs, the top score of the match. The visitors scored 76 and 59, but the European team made 98 in its first innings and was 38 runs for one wicket in its second. Consequently, the Aborigines lost by nine wickets on this occasion. Despite this blow to their prestige, they proved popular and their good behaviour drew favourable comment. Reporting the dinner given by Balmoral citizens, the *Hamilton Spectator* emphasized the poor manners of the Hamilton club, by stressing that at Balmoral '*all* players and their friends' were seated at table. In proposing a toast to the visitors, Officer remarked upon the 'gratification both he and the others felt at the courtesy and gentlemanly demeanor of the Native team, both during play and all the time they were at Balmoral'. Patronizing sentiments though they seem in retrospect, in their contemporary context they were unusual; here also is the first hint that as the team conformed to European ways, they would continue to play together as a club. One guest at the dinner was the local medical practitioner, Dr W. T. Molloy, a person interested in Aboriginal welfare. He was to monitor closely the team's management.[14]

The approaching end to the winter of 1866 brought indications of more ambitious goals for the Aboriginal cricketers.

By August, Hayman had despatched photographs of the team, 'in proper costume and quite civilized in appearance', to Melbourne as a publicity effort. These photographs may be those in Plate 17. When the Melbourne Cricket Club met on 15 November, it considered an application to stage a match between the Aboriginal team and the MCC. It was lodged by Rowland Newbury, 'curator of the pavilion and ground', that is, the proprietor of a refreshment pavilion. Paralleling English professional cricket arrangements, this entrepreneur hoped to gain thirsty and hungry patrons, for which advantage he paid the club £25. As so often happened with the transmission of news by the colonial press, by the time this news item reached the *Hamilton Spectator*, Rowland Newbury had become transformed into 'Rowley'. Not a surprising error, perhaps, as a refreshment tent bearing the name Bryant and Rowley actually served patrons at that fixture (Plate 4). T. W. Wills (who took up his duties at Lake Wallace during late November) was appointed coach.

There is no reason to believe that the promotion of the Melbourne tour was a financial speculation by Hayman or any other Edenhope backer, despite the support of the Melbourne caterer. The Edenhope club members should be credited with altruism and local pride. Donald Cameron, a local squatter, undertook to fill a subscription list to cover the costs of sustaining and clothing the Aborigines while they underwent regular training. Hugh McLeod of Benayeo, near Apsley, who played against them, was the local correspondent for the Victorian Board for the Protection of the Aborigines, and as such assumed some responsibility for their welfare. Hayman and Hamilton gave freely of time to assist the cause. Hayman later denied that he received any remuneration for acting as team manager in Melbourne, and there is no reason to doubt either this or his claim that he had obtained the permission of all settlers with cricketers in their employ to remove the Aborigines from the district.

Despite the paternalistic overtones and the implication that Europeans controlled 'their' Aborigines, neither the activities of the Edenhope supporters nor the reporting of the *Hamilton Spectator* indicate that the Europeans held superior attitudes. Comments are not unduly patronizing and there is no hint of racial discrimination. The newspaper set the tone with its blessing on the project, and its hope that black and white might meet on equal terms.[15] 'That generous kindness of the remote settlers,' it added, 'has disclosed to the outer world a mine of undeniable talent in the aborigine.'

The Edenhope club had attracted the best cricketer in the colony, T. W. Wills (1835–80), who had established his reputation in England between 1853 and 1856. In accepting the offer, Wills must have been reminded of his last experience of Aborigines. Under the circumstances, it was an unusual decision. His pastoralist and parliamentarian father, Horatio Spencer Wills, moved from Victoria in 1860, intending to settle with his family in Queensland. On 17 October 1861 he and 18 other Europeans were massacred by the Aborigines on Cullinlaringo station, on the Nogoa River in the Springsure district of Queensland. It was the greatest killing of white men by black men in Australian history. However, white retaliations soon accounted for more than three times that number of lives. Tom Wills owed his life to his absence collecting stores two days' travel down the track at this time. After this disaster, Tom sought increased police protection, but stayed on as station manager, returning to Victoria in 1864. He was a social personality and there is no evidence of any antagonism between himself and the cricketers. It is reported that Aboriginal employees on his father's Victorian properties had taught Tom spear and boomerang throwing, while he knew some Aboriginal vocabulary. It is possible, however, that his influence off the field may not have been in their best interests. Wills was a heavy drinker, and Edenhope provided full facilities at this time. Alcohol eventually ruined his career and led to his tragic suicide in 1880.[16]

Wills was reported to be setting out for Lake Wallace on 18 August 1866, the Melbourne match being arranged at that stage for early November. The pressing seasonal needs of shearing sheep made it impossible to release team members by that date. Here is a rare hint in the historical record which, together with the employment register of Mount Talbot station, illustrate the importance of Aborigines as a labour force in the pastoral industry during this expansionist gold mining and land development period. The recent publication of William Moodie's memoirs adds further support from this region for their value as shearers.[17] Europeans proved reticent in making public acknowledgment of the role of this cheap labour in assisting the expropriation from the land of those very labourers.

The sheep had been shorn by the middle of November, so the Melbourne Cricket Ground was reserved for a Boxing Day fixture. Wills boarded ship for Portland, *en route* for Lake Wallace, on 20 November. Consequently, by the time he eventually met the team, it is doubtful whether he could have coached them for as much as three weeks before they departed for Melbourne.

Wills soon sent off confident reports of the team's prowess. Actually, the Aborigines were defeated by the local club in their initial encounter. During early December, however, they were victorious against a team of 16 players. The Aborigines scored eight wickets for 170 runs, of which Mullagh contributed 81 not out and Wills did not bat. Lake Wallace club included two Aborigines in its team, Watty and Storekeeper, but the entire team was dismissed for only 34 runs. Mullagh captured six wickets and Wills eight. This victory was followed a week later by a third challenge. In its two innings the Edenhope XVI mustered 95 runs, while the Aborigines rattled up 164 in a single innings. The Aborigines left soon afterwards for Melbourne, with Wills as captain and Hayman as manager. An observer of them at practice noted that they copied both the batting and bowling styles adopted by Wills and that they stood up to hard blows from the ball with 'a total disregard'.

Their appearance at the Melbourne Cricket Ground on Boxing Day 1866 was to prove a determining factor in the lives of many of them. In a well-known etching (Plate 18), this team is pictured standing before a tent from which flutters a flag, bearing the initials A. A. C. (Australian Aboriginal Cricketers?). The team is given as Officer, Sugar, Jellico, Cousins, Neddy, Mullagh, Bullocky, Tarpot, Sundown and Peter; seven of them toured England in 1868. But Sugar, hand in pocket, stooped and slight, had died from causes unknown before Boxing Day. When they took the field, Neddy was omitted and Dick-a-Dick (who located the lost Duff children) and Paddy 'the slogger' took their places. Sugar may have died before the team ever set out for Melbourne. The published sketch of the team must have been prepared in advance, probably from the series of photographs which were sent to Melbourne by Hayman. The models may be those portraits in Plate 17, because close examination indicates that the individuals have the same names and the sketch is virtually a mirror image of those photographs.[18]

Boxing Day was a festive occasion, as 8000 spectators arrived at the Melbourne Cricket Ground and 'the tent set aside for the ladies was crowded during the whole afternoon'. The Aborigines proved nervous before this vociferous crowd, and were flat-footed against the slow bowling (Plate 19). Seven of the team failed to score, while Mullagh's 16 and Bullocky's 14 dominated the total of 39. Their opponents scored 101, Cuzens took six wickets and Mullagh and Wills two wickets each. Their second innings total of 87 was better, and Mullagh contributed 33. They lost the match, but won the hearts of spectators and the good opinion of the sporting critics. Cuzens was dubbed a 'capital' bowler while Mullagh and Bullocky proved 'no mean batsmen'.

A journalist was provoked into Eurocentric speculation by the observation that the despised Aboriginal race had proved capable of mastering English cricket. The match, he noted, 'proved... that the blackfellow has an extra-ordinary readiness for picking up a knowledge of cricket, however deficient he may be in other respects... it is only reasonable to suppose that, if properly managed and instructed, the native race might have been turned to much better account... and that instead of gradually dying off from the face of the earth, they might have become civilized and respectable members of society'.[19]

There is a significant parallel between this racialist assumption of the supreme civilizing role of cricket and the British action in fostering Indian cricket. After its introduction there by British regiments, the game was encouraged officially, because it taught British mores, especially manliness, teamwork and the 'phlegmatic' Anglo-Saxon approach. It was hoped, further, that it would foster communal harmony and bridge the caste system. A spokesman for this imperial ideal was Lord Harris, who later captained the English tourists in Melbourne who played a colonial team which included Mullagh. Harris saw cricket as an 'imperial gospel', which mirrored the best English values (and therefore it constituted the acme of civilization).[20]

The smart appearance and determination of the Aboriginal team upon their arrival in Melbourne had impressed members of the Melbourne Cricket Club. Several of their best players were in Sydney for the intercolonial fixture, also set for Boxing Day. After seeing the Aborigines practising, the club acted at once to strengthen their weakened Melbourne team by adding James, a fine slow bowler. This proved to be a crucial decision. In any case, appearances were deceptive. Although Mullagh still managed to perform as the most accomplished player, he was severely hampered by a deeply cut finger. However, an even more significant psychological factor must be considered. The recent death of Sugar, perhaps far from his clan homeland, must have lowered team morale. It seems probable that Sugar also may have been kinsman to some players. Under these circumstances, they did well to dismiss their opponents for only 101 runs, while the standard of their fielding remained brisk.

That the Melbourne Cricket Club, with hindsight, judged this match to have been important may be inferred from its annual report presented during 1867. It observed that 'the season was enlivened...by a match between the Club and Eleven Aborigines of the colony, a sight which appeared to create almost as much excitement as did the first "All English Eleven" matches'.

A grandly titled match was scheduled for the following day: 'Australian natives versus the world'. Wills and four of his team were classified as 'natives' (Australian-born) for the occasion. The third day was devoted to a sports meetings, in which Tarpot, Jellico and Mullagh were prominent. Tarpot ran the 100 yards *backwards* in 14 seconds and probably still retains the Australian title for this unorthodox event. Indeed, Tarpot was the popular hero, and illness which prevented his sailing to England in 1868 robbed the team of a great draw-card. As a critic observed, 'he can jump well, run well, turn a somersault, and be merry on all occasions'. Tarpot turned a double somersault in delight when Officer held a good catch at long leg, perhaps the first foretaste of modern over-exuberance on the field.

The other lively team member, Jellico, was a casualty of the forthcoming tour. Evidently a youthful humorist, he endeared himself to the crowd and a newspaper thought him worth featuring under the heading 'black jokes'. When a European addressed him in broken English, Jellico was reported as responding 'what for you no talk to me good Inglis. I speak him as good Inglis belonging you'. Turning to Tarpot, he observed, 'big one fool that fellow. He not know him Inglis one dam'. When somebody else suggested that he ask Wills to teach him to read and write, he retorted: 'What's usy Wills. He too much along of us. He speak nothing now but blackfellow talk.' Then there was the comment about Melbourne's scorching heat attributed to him: 'I spoil my complexion. When I go back my mother won't know me.'

On the last day of the year, the team relaxed at the Fitzroy bowling green in Victoria Parade. Hayman's men, bewhiskered and garbed in the best Victorian manner, disported themselves with decorum on their day off. Although they were unfamiliar with bowls, Tarpot, Jellico and Dick-a-Dick all impressed club members with their skill. Three weeks later Bullocky and Cuzens made cricket history by becoming the first of their race to play intercolonial cricket. They represented Victoria at the MCG against Tasmania. Cuzens took two wickets, but the Victorians lost, with Cuzens contributing only 4 and 3 and Bullocky 4 and 0. It was a humble opening. It might have been better if Mullagh had played. He was selected but was injured and Bullocky replaced him.

Meanwhile, the sympathetic Melbourne correspondent of the *Hamilton Spectator* made a sober and prophetic assessment of future prospects. In complimenting the team, he trusted that Hayman's influence would 'prevent them from running riot at the public-houses'. Observing that a well-'deserved profit had been made', he added, 'I trust the Aboriginals will reap some substantial benefit from the cash they have helped to earn'. The sad reality is that three of the Aborigines died, possibly as a direct consequence of the tour.[21]

NOTES

[1] The only sources touching directly on the area from which the team was recruited are: J. C. Hamilton, *Pioneering Days in Western Victoria* (Melbourne, 1912), 33–40; T. F. Bride (ed.), *Letters from Victorian Pioneers* (Melbourne, 1898), 177. Kangaroo hunts: *H.S.*, 5 September 1866; 17 August and 9 November 1867. There is an excellent summary

of Aboriginal plant foods by Beth Gott, 'Murnong — *Microseris scapigera*: a study of a staple food of Victorian Aborigines', *Australian Aboriginal Studies*, 2 (1983): 2–18.

[2] The Lake Condah fish traps have been surveyed by Coutts, P. J. F., *et al*, *Aboriginal Engineers of the Western District, Victoria* (Melbourne, 1978). For a discussion of eel fisheries and population estimates of western Victoria, see the innovative articles by Harry Lourandos, 'Aboriginal spatial organization and population', *Archaeology and Physical Anthropology in Australia*, 12 (1977): 202–25, and 'Change or stability?: hydraulics, hunter-gatherers and population in temperate Australia', *World Archaeology*, 11 (1980): 245–64.

[3] The 1863 population estimate is given in R. Brough Smyth, *The Aborigines of Victoria* (Melbourne, 1978), vol 1, 43; that by Hamilton, in *Pioneering Days*, 96.

[4] The limited availability of cricketers: *Aust.*, 9 February, 171, and 16 February 1867, 203. The reference to the *Handbook of Victoria* (London, 1886), 23.

[5] Conditions in the Western District: the petition is an Uncatalogued MS, Dixson Library, Sydney — various documents listed under 'Aborigines'; esp. March 1842, and various reports by Dana, 1842–43. Chauncey diaries: Dixson MSS, no 338, entry for 29 February 1848.

[6] See M. F. Christie, *Aborigines in Colonial Victoria 1835–86* (Melbourne, 1979), 62, 75–6. The recent survey of violent deaths is by Beverley Nance, 'The level of violence: European and Aborigines in Port Phillip, 1835–1850', *Historical Studies* 19 (1981): 532–52; Peter Corris, *Aborigines and Europeans in Western Victoria* (Canberra, 1968), 157.

[7] The shepherd was described by C. B. Hall in T. F. Bride (ed.), *Letters from Victorian Pioneers* (Melbourne, 1898), 217–18. For H.S. Wills, Corris, 90, 99.

[8] Hamilton's account of the massacre, *Pioneering Days*, 34.

[9] The western settlements are reconstructed from *H.S.* files, which also describes the Duff saga in August–September 1864, esp. 7 and 14 September. L. J. Blake, *Lost in the Bush* (Melbourne, 1964) covers the whole story. The Edenhope cricket club and Hayman's involvement derive from *H.S.*, esp. 2 March 1867.

[10] An account of J. B. Fitzgerald and of Mullagh and Pine Hill station transactions is provided by S. M. Ingham, *Enterprising Migrants* (Melbourne, 1975), 137–47. We are indebted for personal advice to Mr David Edgar, Nerrinyerie, and Mr S. Sondhu, Mullagh.

[11] For permission to use Mount Talbot station records, we thank Mr and Mrs D. Officer, Toolondo. C. M. Officer is described in *Australian*

Dictionary of Biography (*A.D.B.*) vol 5, 357–8; his association with the Upper Glenelg club — *H.S.*, 4 April 1866; an anonymous letter in *H.S.*, 6 February 1867, asserted that Officer coached Bullocky.

[12] Cuzens and the hurdle bar: a comment by Hayman, *H.S.*, 16 February 1867. Hayman's songs: *H.S.*, 25 July 1899. Tom Hamilton's career draws upon Hamilton, *Pioneering Days*, 82; *H.S.*, 6 February 1867; his letter in Hayman's defence, *H.S.*, 2 March 1867.

[13] Some participants in the first match were listed in a letter from A. A. Cowell, *H.S.*, 27 August 1891. Further details concerning the team's formation — Hamilton, *Pioneering Days*, 82; *H.S.*, 27 January 1866, 6 and 16 February, 2 March 1867.

[14] The Hamilton and Balmoral matches are described in *H.S.*, 27 January, 21 and 24 March, 4 April 1866.

[15] The background to the Melbourne tour is from *H.S.*, 15, 18, 25 August 1866; *Aust.*, 4 May 1867.

[16] For the massacre, see D. Carment, 'The Wills massacre of 1861: Aboriginal–European Conflict on the Colonial Australian Frontier', *Journal of Australian Studies*, 6 (1980): 49–55. For Tom Wills, see *A.D.B.*, 6: 409–10, and Dunstan, *The Paddock that Grew*, 19–20.

[17] *W. Moodie: A Pioneer of Western Victoria*, ed. J. A. Palmer (Melbourne, 1973), 73.

[18] The Melbourne visit is covered by *H.S.*, 12, 19, 26 December 1866, 2 January 1867; *Australian News* (Melbourne), 20 December 1866, 1, 10; the team illustration was prepared for *Illustrated Melbourne Post*, 24 January 1867.

[19] The fullest account is provided by *Aust.*, 18 August, 8 September, 27 October, 24 November, 8, 29 December 1866 (for Eurocentric speculation).

[20] Indian cricket: R. Cashman, in R. Cashman and M. McKernan (eds.), *Sport in History* (St Lucia, 1979), 189–90.

[21] MCC Minutes, 15 November, 11 December 1866; Annual Report MCC, 1867, 28. Jellico's 'black jokes': *H.S.*, 23 January 1867, quoting the *Bendigo Advertiser*. The prophetic comment: *H.S.*, 2 January 1867.

3

The Sydney Tour 1867

An alert Sydney visitor, 'Captain' W. E. B. Gurnett (or W. E. Broughton-Gurnett), was an interested spectator at the Boxing Day match. Although he posed as a man of substance, Sydney directories and newspapers are curiously reticent about Gurnett's activities. However, the fact that he lived in a boarding house at an imposing address, 219 Macquarie Street, does nothing to confirm his financial solidity. He must have possessed the fluent tongue common to confidence tricksters, and could spin more than a cricket ball.

Gurnett approached Hayman and Wills and convinced them that they had a potential fortune within their guardianship. He may have involved himself in team affairs a month previously. The *Australasian* carried an enigmatic item on 8 December 1866. It reported news of the team from Lake Wallace, citing Wills as its source: 'It appears that some speculator is at work trying to upset present arrangements, and secure the blacks for his own ends.'[1]

Wills had close contact with the cricket correspondent 'Longstop', W. T. Hammersley, who was a friend of long standing. They had sailed from England together in 1856, Hammersley had preceded Wills as captain of the Victorian colonial team and they both collaborated in initiating the game of Australian Rules football. Consequently, 'Longstop' was well placed to field news from Lake Wallace.

Gurnett proposed a 12-month cricket tour to Sydney and England, during which he would finance the team's wages, expenses and clothing, together with those of the captain and manager. On their return, each Aboriginal would receive a

£50 bonus, and Wills a larger sum; the fortunate Hayman would take a percentage of the profits. Gurnett undertook to make all shipping and other business arrangements. Youthful and gullible Hayman and professional sportsman Wills gladly signed the proffered contract, while 12 dark cricketers affixed their marks. Later events labelled Gurnett a plausible rogue, but his motivation is obscure. He evidently lacked capital, and perhaps gambled on making a small fortune from the team's Australian games, which he could plough back to finance the overseas tour. Presumably, Gurnett was familiar with the profits made by All-England XI tours, and the cash flow from thousands of Melbourne Cricket Ground patrons must have tempted him to attempt a tour in reverse direction. Hayman found that city business methods were more complex than affairs in Edenhope. Despite a sincere and sustained concern for the welfare of his charges, he showed little business sense.

With a long tour planned, Hayman had to take immediate action to enlarge the team. By 8 January he had applied to the Melbourne Cricket Club for a return game. In order to give him the necessary time, matches were arranged also at Collingwood, Geelong, Ballarat and Bendigo during January and a farewell appearance at the MCG was scheduled for 8 February. This schedule also allowed time for Bullocky and Cuzens to play in the intercolonial match against Tasmania. During the first week of January, the crowd and cricketers at the Geelong match proved so law-abiding that Sergeant McSweeney's smartly turned out police troop was not required, although the Volunteer Artillery band was well received. More interest was shown in the athletics meeting than in the rather weak cricket, for the home team scored 25 and 37 respectively in its two innings. Mullagh top scored with 49 and four other Aborigines reached double figures in the total of 170. Meanwhile, Hayman hastened homewards, and was reported in Hamilton by 16 January, on his mission to recruit three additional players.

In an apologia written to the press some weeks later, Hayman claimed that he contacted all settlers on stations supplying team members, and that their permission was sought to allow the tour to proceed. It was granted, on the condition that Hayman always travelled with the team. It is interesting to consider the implications of this procedure. While paternalistic, and indicating a concern for their welfare, the attitudes of both Hayman and the squatters presupposed a proprietorial interest in 'their' Aborigines; they were part of the station property. Although he made no reference to any government instrumentality or legal authority, Hayman's actions were definitely within the bounds of contemporary colonial legislation regarding native peoples.

It is relevant to consider, also, that these Aboriginal men probably did regard themselves as 'belonging' to specific stations, although for different reasons than European proprietorship. Most of them were living on their traditional lands, so they had no wish to leave when pastoralists occupied the area. The tragic saga of the displacement of these western Victorian people was beginning, with their compulsory removal to distant missions or government settlements. As most of such settlements date from the late 1860s, it is likely that in early 1867 most Aborigines still lived on or near their traditional territories. The fact that many of them worked on pastoral properties may indicate that, during these years when gold fever still attracted many Europeans, Aboriginal labour proved valuable to the pastoralists who, only two decades earlier, had occupied their land by force.

The tour continued on 11–12 January 1867 against a muster of 15 members of Collingwood's Prince of Wales club on the Heidelberg road. Although this loyal club's president was Graham Berry, a future premier, and its secretary was Gambling, fortune did not favour the hosts. The visitors scored 136, of which 50 runs came from Mullagh's bat, while their 15 opponents totalled 81. Wills collected 10 wickets, eight of them bowled.

The victors shifted operations to Bendigo with their ranks depleted through illness. John Conway, the Melbourne cricketer who later conceived the idea of sending the first white Australian team to England, joined Wills in playing for the Aborigines. Their team scored 84 runs in the first innings thanks to Wills and Mullagh, the latter still recovering from illness. Wills took seven wickets in the Bendigo first innings and combined with Mullagh to take a further seven in the second. This sufficed to defeat the Bendigo United Club, whose wicket-keeper also contributed substantially to their defeat by allowing 25 byes (only a single bye was credited to the Aborigines).

The Bendigo XI included two teenagers who were later to make names for themselves in Test cricket. William Evans Midwinter was only 15 at the time, but he eventually became the only person in Test cricket history to play for both Australia (1878–84) and England (1881–82). Henry Frederick Boyle's round-arm, medium-paced bowling teamed with Spofforth to become the first great bowling combination. Their greatest triumph was at the Oval in 1882, where they routed the English team and created the legend of the Ashes. All this was ahead of the two youths, however, when they played the Aborigines. Midwinter took four wickets, but otherwise their performances were undistinguished.

Their Ballarat excursion was unsuccessful. The local team won by 10 wickets, after scoring 108 in its first innings, while the Aborigines struggled to compile 42 and 71 in their two appearances at the crease (Plate 23). Social activities proved more rewarding, when the team patronized the Theatre Royal to watch the 'drama', a joint billing of 'Rip Van Winkle' and 'Nan, the Good for Nothing'. This spectacle concluded, they applauded their mate Cuzens, who stepped on stage to receive a bat and a purse subscribed for his match performance. Cuzens was fortunate, because he captured only one wicket and made scores of 7 and 26, inferior to the six wickets and 51 runs contributed by his captain, Wills.[2]

Advertisements appeared on 2 February announcing the return match at the Melbourne Cricket Ground, to be played a week later. It was stated that the team was to proceed immediately to Sydney, and ultimately sail to Panama and on to England. It seems a most improbable route, at a period before the Panama Canal existed. There were rumours, also, that the term would play in Brisbane. It was all very vague; only one of several indications that the enterprise was not being well planned. In the first place, there was the matter of Mr Gurnett's cheques — they 'bounced'. Despite Gurnett's protestations to the contrary, the *Age* reported that some cheques signed by Gurnett as payment for expenses incurred on the team's Bendigo visit had been dishonoured. His creditors had taken out a writ to prevent him from leaving the colony on 11 February. Before that date, however, Gurnett had made an acceptable 'proposal for a composition' and departed for Sydney.

There was also the problem of the attitude of the Melbourne Cricket Club, the spectators at its ground and the issue of team morale. The crowd which had lionized the Aborigines six weeks earlier only turned out in small numbers to witness their return appearance. When it was time to take the field only two members of the MCC team were at the ground, and a scratch muster, which was dubbed the 'County of Bourke' XI, provided the balance of the opposition. Although the MCC minute book reveals no indifference to the match, the press noted that some players could not have time off work to play. Whatever the cause, something (not the weather) restricted the attendance. The Aborigines won the match, but not convincingly for a vaunted touring side. It was observed that they 'played very carelessly'. They made 154 in their first innings, of which Wills contributed 37, but they allowed the weak scratch team to reach 151 runs. The Aborigines performed better in the second innings, thanks to Cuzens who made 49 of their 134, and he took four wickets to dismiss the opposition for 70 runs. As the Melbourne team bowled underarm, the Aboriginal success was not overwhelming. Undaunted by his difficulties, Gurnett was on hand to introduce his men personally to the governor, who praised their play and presented a bat to Cuzens as a reward for prowess. He also watched the game, and saw one of the newcomers, 'Paddy the slogger, hit away hard and fast'.

Team health was a worry and it was opportune that Hayman's reinforcements arrived in time for the MCG game. Mullagh was unable to play because of injury, Tarpot had a severe cold, while Dick-a-Dick was suffering from measles, that terrible scourge of Aboriginal Australians. In the light of later developments, it is possible that the falling off in playing standard resulted from excessive drinking.[3]

After their appearance at Ballarat, the *Ballarat Star* made some pertinent comments in a long and sympathetic editorial. It urged Wills to coach the team further before tempting fate by challenging more powerful English teams, such as the All-England XI. It also expected the government to 'exact proper guaranties [*sic*] of their due protection abroad and their return...within the stipulated period', and added, 'some people no doubt will tempt the blacks to drink'.

Quite apart from Gurnett's financial difficulties, the proposed colonial and overseas tour also was in jeopardy from unexpected quarters. On 12 February only two days before the team left for Sydney, an attempt was made at official level to prevent the tour taking place. The Central Board for the Protection of the Aborigines held a special meeting, and its secretary wrote an 'urgent and immediate' note to the Chief Secretary of Victoria requesting government intervention.

The Central Board for the Protection of the Aborigines had been established by the governor's decree in 1860, as a result of a Select Committee Report of the Victorian Parliament on Aboriginal welfare. The board only received statutory authority under the Aboriginal Protection Act in 1869. At the time of this tour, it consisted of seven members, including parliamentary representatives and others whose interests lay in the mission field or with a humanitarian concern for social welfare. R. Brough Smyth, a public servant, was appointed secretary of the central board which maintained a system of honorary correspondents throughout the colony to publicize or implement board activities. Smyth was primarily a geologist and mineralogist, but his name is best remembered for his massive two-volume *The Aborigines of Victoria*, a basic corpus of ethnographic data, which he published a decade later.

In his note to the chief secretary, Brough Smyth explained that the board had no personal knowledge of the organizers of the tour, but acknowleged that the Aborigines were 'skilful cricketers'. They were concerned in case the players might be abandoned and left destitute in England. Unless the promoters left a sufficient guarantee of their bona fides, the board requested immediate action by the governor to stop the tour. The sum deposited should be adequate to ensure the team's safe return home. Not unreasonably, Brough Smyth observed that the board sought 'to prevent this simple people from falling into the hands of those who have not up to the present time shown that they have sought their intercourse with other than purely mercenary ends in view'.

The chief secretary replied by return post, in an essentially negative vein. He regretted that neither the governor nor the government 'have any legal power to compel persons who are taking the Aboriginals to England to give any such guarantee as it proposed. If the Central Board can suggest any legal course by which their object can be accomplished the Chief Secretary will be glad to adopt it'.

An appeal for official intervention was launched independently in the press by an anonymous letter-writer, who claimed that the Aborigines would perish from diseases contracted on tour. As the author of this letter claimed to know team members, it was almost certainly Dr W. T. Molloy, the Balmoral doctor who was active on this same theme at a later stage. Indeed, it was probably Molloy who alerted Brough Smyth to the situation in the first place, because he was the board's voluntary correspondent in Balmoral.

Gurnett must have taken successful evasive action to mollify the central board, as the tour was not referred to again in board minutes. Indeed, word spread that the board had received a bond for the safe return of the team. The *Age* reported that the sum was £1000. But someone was misinformed, because Gurnett was unlikely to possess such a sum. The cricket editor of the *Australasian*, who believed that the amount was £500, later questioned whether it ever had been paid — 'it is to be hoped the matter will be looked into by the authorities'. If a bond was paid, there is no mention of it in the record.[4]

When the Aborigines first appeared in Sydney, their standard of play had not improved. On 21 February, they began their two-day match against the Albert Club, Redfern, on a ground swallowed by housing development in later years but at this time Sydney's major venue (Plate 20), having been opened in 1864. The team led by Wills included Bullocky, Cuzens, Dick-a-Dick, Jellico, Mullagh, Paddy, Peter, Harry Rose, Tarpot and Watty (Plates 21 & 22).

The Governor of New South Wales was in attendance and although the Aborigines proved 'moderately' proficient as round-arm bowlers, they were slow in the field and lost the match by 132 runs. Wills proved to be the only successful player with both bat and ball. The press was unimpressed by their prowess and the great Caffyn scorned their abilities to such an extent that he challenged the entire team to play him at single wicket cricket, but the game never took place. The athletics meeting held on the third day pleased the 8000 spectators who had paid their one shilling or half-crown admittance fee. The Aborigines performed well in sports, and Dick-a-Dick threw a cricket ball 114 yards.

This throw was the best recorded by any Aboriginal, even

on the English tour, although it was not a record. A throw of 122 yards by a European was recorded in New South Wales and Spofforth achieved a distance of 120 yards. According to sporting tradition, a throw of 140 yards was achieved in 1872 by Billy, a Queensland Aboriginal from Brisbane. It was measured by Donald Wallace, an MCC committeeman and owner of the famous racehorse Carbine, but *Wisden* refused to allow this record.[5]

There was an unscheduled event on the first day of the match, the details of which were unfortunately unreported. Play stopped while Wills (the captain) and Hayman (an umpire) 'were arrested at the suit of Mr Jarrett [Gurnett] for alleged breach of contract...Messrs O'Brien (Tattersall's) and Lawrence (the cricketer) became security for them, and they were at once released, and the game proceeded'. Lawrence's action was the first development in his long association with the Aboriginal cricketers. His initial contact with the team may have been due to Wills and himself renewing contact, since they played together in the All-Ireland XI in 1854, a subject discussed later.

It is difficult to get at the truth of this matter, because the papers proved so reticent. Even the *Hamilton Spectator*, which had expressed interest in the team before its departure, preserved silence on its activities throughout the months from February to May. The first news was a short announcement that the team was returning home, because 'it is evident that [Hayman] and his blacks entrusted themselves into hands which were not quite trustworthy'. This would seem to be a mild understatement, if Hayman's own testimony is accepted. Gurnett must have defaulted in some manner and this trumped-up legal action was a subterfuge to cover himself. Gurnett once again wrote a letter full of moral indignation to the press, putting forward his case, but his explanation was implausible. Meantime, Hayman claimed that he had never received any payment from Gurnett, and had been forced to dip into his own limited resources; passages had not been reserved on the ship, despite Gurnett's statement that they had.

For some weeks, Hayman attempted to come to an agreement, but without success, as Gurnett probably intended. It was an impasse. As Wills and Hayman were contracted to Gurnett, even if they had been able to raise funds independently, they could not depart. A report in the *Queenslander*, on 13 April, stated that 'Gurnett threatened to arrest them if they attempted to do so'. It must be inferred from the same report that the anxious promoters of an anticipated Brisbane fixture on 6 April telegraphed a Sydney shipping office to ascertain whether the team had sailed. On receipt of a negative response, they cancelled the engagement.[6]

The team was stranded by the end of February, not overseas as the Central Board for the Protection of the Aborigines feared, but in Sydney. While awaiting clarification of the legal situation, Hayman and Wills evidently decided to defray costs by staging further matches. During the first week of March, games were played at Maitland (lost) and Newcastle (drawn), but with a financial loss, because it had cost £50 to stage the games and the proceeds totalled a meagre £14. More significantly, in explaining the team's poor performance at Maitland, the local paper noted that 'several' of the team were 'not in good health'. At Newcastle a few days later Rose suffered from a 'violent cold', while other team members also were 'seriously ill'. Even so, the Aboriginal competitors won all the prizes in the athletic events and the same correspondent commended their 'spruce' appearance, including those wearing 'lavender kid gloves'. The team won a one-day fixture at the Albert ground during mid-March and drew another rain-interrupted match there. A one-day fixture was arranged at Manly Beach for 16 March, with a possible follow-up on 23 March, which was won by the Aborigines. Playing for Manly was G. Smith, a future backer of the English tour. At this time, Lawrence was the licensee of the Pier Hotel, on Manly's Esplanade, so probably he arranged that fixture. Perhaps he also staged the following engagement, at Wollongong on 5–6 April. Not only did he play in the team there, together with Wills and nine Aborigines, but he captained the team instead of Wills. His assumption of responsibilities was the forerunner of deeper involvement. Charley Dumas, an hitherto unreported Aboriginal cricketer, made his first appearance at Wollongong, where he stood as an umpire. A report a year later stated that Charley came from New South Wales, so it is possible that he was a player known to Lawrence, who brought him along in case of need. Whatever the facts of the situation, Charley did not return with the team to Edenhope, although he joined the second team at Geelong, as a late replacement, before they sailed for overseas.[7]

Bad weather intervened to ruin the team's financial prospects against Wollongong's Illawarra club. Rain on the first day restricted attendance and torrential overnight rains turned the wicket into a quagmire for the second day. The fact that there was a brick pit nearby indicates that this was a quality sticky wicket. The Aboriginal team fortunately batted on the first day, scoring 116, and then bundled out their opposition next day for 20 runs, whereupon no further play was possible. Lawrence opened and was the first man out for 5 runs; Cuzens made only 8, but he was singled out for his 'masterly dexterity' by the local reporter. Wills was 27 not out, but Mullagh's 45 was so stylish that his innings was considered to have been 'never surpassed' on that ground. Wills and Lawrence shared all the bowling, capturing five wickets each.

Despite the conditions, a sports exhibition followed. It started with boomerang throwing, but this had to be abandoned for safety reasons because the crowd surged forward into the firing line. The high jump was completed without incident, with five of the team bettering the best jump of local challengers, while Dick-a-Dick cleared the bar at 5 feet 4 inches. Tarpot was winning the footrace, when a Wollongong competitor was 'guilty of as cool and deliberate a jostle as was ever witnessed'. In the face of such unruly crowd behaviour, the visitors showed their independence by refusing to compete further and they 'quietly left the ground'.

Regardless of weather and incidents, Lawrence may have found his time spent with the team an intriguing financial prospect. On the positive side Mullagh and Cuzens looked players of class; Lawrence probably had encountered fewer more natural sportsmen during his period in Australia. Several Aborigines were sufficiently athletic to defeat Europeans at their own sports, to which they added skills in their tribal arts, obviously a popular novelty with spectators. Lawrence may have agreed with the paternalistic but appreciative local newspaper reporter who perceived 'a general and admired proficiency... [which] proves beyond a doubt that the Aboriginal natives of this country are capable of learning the arts and sciences of civilized life if the trouble were taken to cultivate this latent and neglected talent'. A Britisher of his time, he confirmed that 'civilized life' and cricket were identical concepts by illustrating Aboriginal potential by reference to 'the professional air and bearing of Charley [Dumas] in the capacity of umpire'. As Lawrence received an advance payment on 20 July to cover his travel to Edenhope and he arrived there to coach the team by mid-August, he surely must have discussed the proposed overseas tour with Hayman and Graham in Sydney during April.

When the team returned to Sydney from Wollongong, an immediate decision must have been taken to abandon plans for the current tour. At least that follows from the Queensland telegram of 6 April, discussed previously. Hayman was faced with the pressing problem of funding their return to Victoria. At Parramatta on 9–10 April, they challenged a Cumberland County XI, but lost, despite major efforts by Wills and Lawrence, who scored 57 runs and captured 17 wickets between them. Lawrence and other supporters undertook to arrange a benefit match at the Albert ground, whose trustees agreed to waive all fees. In spite of this consideration, the proceeds of the game proved insufficient to pay even their fares to Melbourne, since bad weather continued to dog the team. It was an Easter-time fixture, but conditions were exceptionally bleak and the Aborigines lost by 15 runs. Possibly Hayman paid the necessary balance on transport home, because he claimed a personal loss of £400 on the tour. Lawrence may have provided further support out of self-interest, however, because by now his future must have seemed to lie with the team.[8]

Charles Lawrence (1828–1917) was well adapted to see financial possibilities in an All-Aboriginal XI. His invitation to tour Victoria with the first All-England XI in 1861 was no chance, for he had an impressive record as a tough professional. He enjoyed cricket and was above average as an all-rounder. As a Surrey schoolboy he played truant to see the batting hero of his day, Fuller Pilch (he arrived at Lord's after hitching a ride in a dog cart, only to see his hero out to the first ball). As a youth he played in Perth, Scotland, later combining duties on a railway station with frequent cricket. He was selected in a team to play William Clarke's All-England XI at Edinburgh in 1849, and captured all 10 wickets in an innings for 53 runs. Clarke subsequently obtained a professional appointment for him, in 1851, with Dublin's Phoenix club. He remained in Ireland for a decade, being appointed cricketing coach to two successive Lords-Lieutenant of Ireland and forming a professional United All-Ireland XI. It is interesting to note that, in 1854, T. W. Wills journeyed to Ireland, evidently with a Liverpool team, which defeated the Phoenix Club. Wills took 10 wickets with his round-arm deliveries, whereupon Lawrence selected him to play in his All-Ireland XI for one match.

As Lawrence maintained contacts with England, his invitation to leave Ireland and join the Australian tour was natural. Lawrence's career was opportunistic, so his decision to remain in Australia is understandable, as was his later identification with the fortunes of the Aborigines. It is worth remarking, also, that he was an optimist rather than a canny businessman. On his own admission, a tennis court which he established in Dublin 'was not a success'. When he arranged his own benefit match in Phoenix Park, the wind blew all the elaborate and expensive tents and canvas field barriers away and he lost on the event.[9]

If there is a question mark concerning Lawrence's business acumen, doubts about William Hayman's managerial abilities must be raised even more emphatically. He had been swayed easily by Gurnett at Christmas time; by Easter he had changed backers, evidently with equal enthusiasm. Hayman was young, celebrating his 26th birthday during this tour. He also was an inexperienced 'new chum', whose uncle at Lake Wallace South station may have set an unbusiness-like example. Family tradition maintains that J. P. Hayman lived well, but beyond his means. As a consequence, he was forced to sell Lake Wallace South in 1868.

Whatever the source of the funds for the Aboriginal team's passage to Melbourne, the members arrived back there destitute at the beginning of May. In order to assist them, a successful athletics meeting was staged at the MCG on 4 May. The profits were entrusted to Hayman for the team's fares home, a gesture which elicted a letter of thanks from Hayman to the MCC secretary. He immediately wrote a touching letter to the press 'to tender my sincere thanks to the public, both in Sydney and Melbourne for the sympathy and support I have received...and I am happy to state that I am now in a position to take the aboriginal cricketers to their homes'. That week they sailed to Portland, where they played a game on 9 May. Tom Hamilton joined the team there and under his captaincy the Aborigines defeated a Portland XVII. Because the Hamilton club ignored a suggestion that it might challenge the team on its way home, the players returned direct to Edenhope, where they dispersed.[10]

The abortive international tour had ended. Hayman stated

that he lost £400; presumably Wills also suffered financially. Wills's connection with the team terminated in Melbourne where he coached during the next season. Because this first tour has been telescoped by commentators with the 1868 venture, many writers have credited Wills with taking the team to England, or at least with coaching them for longer than he actually did. He was associated with the team for about five months. Wills was a great cricket coach and must have taught the Aborigines a great deal about the game. However, as a heavy drinker, he was probably not a good influence for them off the field.

The personal cost of the tour to the cricketers was incalculable. Sugar was dead before their first match; Watty (a replacement) died on the road home; Jellico and the exuberant Paddy died from pneumonia soon after arriving back; Harry Rose, Tarpot and Dick-a-Dick had been seriously ill; team members received no payment for their services. The cricket historian, A. G. Moyes, who was unaware of these melancholy particulars, commented on members of the first tour that 'many failed to make the team for England'. The reason is obvious. It was appropriate that the lusty hitter, Paddy, made his last cricket appearance at Portland and top scored with 21 runs.

Poor Watty was only 25 kilometres from Edenhope, near Kadnook, when he died in the cart. An inquest was held at the Lake Wallace Hotel and both the testimony provided, and varied interpretations placed upon it, are relevant. Watty, a heavy drinker, had become drunk at Portland, and again at Coleraine. After eating a hearty breakfast the next morning, he died suddenly, while lying on the floor of the cart. Medical examination established that his lungs were diseased. In assenting to a verdict of death due to discharge from the lungs, neither the jury nor the newspaper reporter felt constrained to pass any moral censure on Watty's alcoholism or the role of his European guardians.

Mounted Constable Thomas Kennedy, a discerning and

literate officer, interpreted the evidence differently. In his opinion, lung failure was a consequential and not causative factor. He later wrote to his superintendent at Portland that the significant evidence adduced at the inquest was that Watty 'as well as others of the team were continually drunk'. Alcohol and the unusual living conditions encountered on tour explained why so many Aborigines had died. Independent substantiation of Kennedy's claim that other team members drank heavily may be inferred from an unsolicited testimonial in the *Australasian*, which praised Dick-a-Dick's firm advocacy of temperance, and the fine example which he set his less abstemious mates. 'He had a horror of drunkenness and visited anyone who indulged...with...punishment.' Billy Officer, another member of this team, was involved at a later date in court proceedings against an Edenhope pub-keeper who sold him grog. Indeed, alcohol ruined the lives of other team members in later years. In his report, the realistic police officer noted the tragic truth, that grog was a 'potent reasoner' with Aborigines. It must have been a dispirited team which disbanded in Edenhope during mid-May.[11]

NOTES

[1] The role of Gurnett and the formation of the team to tour abroad is based upon Hayman's own explanation, *Aust.*, 4 May 1867, 555. Other sources are *Aust.*, 23 February, 27 April, and 11 May 1867; *H.S.*, 12, 16 January 1867; *Argus*, 5 January 1867. The enigmatic comment: *Aust.*, 8 December 1866, 1132.

[2] The Melbourne match and other Victorian fixtures: *Age*, 9, 11 and 25 February 1867; *H.S.*, 13 February 1867; *Aust.*, 9 February 1867; *Argus*, 11 February 1867; *Ballarat Star*, 1–2, 4 February 1867.

[3] Gurnett's cheques and character, *Age*, 14 and 15 February 1867. However, there is no reference to these matters in the report on the match in the *Bendigo Advertiser*, 6 January 1867. The MCC advertisement and Panama route: *Aust.*, 2 February 1867, 139; Brisbane, *Queenslander*, 13 April 1867, 8, a reference which we owe to Ms G. Blades.

[4] The evidence for official intervention is contained in the following sources: Minutes of the Central Board Appointed to Watch Over the Interests of the Aborigines, vol 1, folio, special meeting 12 February 1867 (Aborigines Welfare Board, Victoria); Chief Secretary's Papers; Letters inwards, 12 February 1867, 1548; Letter outwards, 13 February 1867, 324 — a folio volume, January 1866–May 1867 (State Library of Victoria, Archives). Dr Molloy's intervention: *Aust.*, 9 February 1867, 172. Newspaper comment on the bond: *Age*, 25 February 1867; *Aust.*, 27 April 1867, 524.

[5] Throwing the cricket ball was an important contest in the late nineteenth century. A number of the Aborigines were capable of reaching 100 yards. For the Sydney match, *S.M.H.*, 22, 23 and 25 February 1867; Dick-a-Dick, 25 February. Spofforth: H. Heaton, *Australian Dictionary of Dates and Men of the Time* (Sydney, 1879), part 2, 79. For Billy's 140 yards throw: Arthur Haygarth, *Cricket Scores and Biographies*. Hugh Field, pers. comm. believed that Billy came from Charleville.

[6] Gurnett and legal action: *Aust.*, 23 February 1867; *Age*, 22 February 1867. The later sequence of events is based upon *H.S.*, 8 May 1867; *Aust.*, 4 May 1867; *Age*, 27 April 1867; *Queenslander*, 13 April 1867, 8.

[7] The NSW fixtures were described in *Aust.*, 16 March 1867; *S.M.H.*, 6, 13, 18, 19 March 1867; *Maitland Mercury*, 2, 5 March 1867, 4; *Illawarra Mercury*, 9 April 1867; A. P. Fleming, *The International Aboriginal Cricketers v. Illawarra* (Wollongong, 1968). We acknowledge the assistance of Mr Fleming in researching the Wollongong episode. The newspaper reports on the Wollongong match are reproduced in Fleming's booklet. Charley Dumas was stated to come from NSW in an issue of the *Field*, October 1868 (Graham, Accounts, 335).

[8] Funding the return home: *Aust.*, 27 April and 4 May 1867.

[9] The summary of Lawrence's career is based upon manuscripts in his own writing in the possession of Ian Friend. See also *Wisden* (1920), 230, and W. P. Hone, *Cricket in Ireland* (Tralee, 1955), 16. Reference to Lawrence's receipt of funds to travel to Edenhope is provided in G. W. Graham's account book, for which see Ch. 4.

[10] The team in Melbourne and the way home: *Argus*, 4 May 1867; *Aust.*, 11 May 1867; *H.S.*, 11 May 1867; MCC Minutes, 14 May 1867.

[11] Death of Jellico: Hamilton, *Pioneering Days*, 81; Watty: *H.S.*, 22 May 1867; Chief Secretary's Papers — Letters inwards, an enclosure with a letter by R. Brough Smyth, 14 October 1867, no 210514 (State Library of Victoria, Archives); Dick-a-Dick and temperance: *Aust.*, 11 May 1867, 588; Billy Officer: *H.S.*, 5 February 1868. The comment by A. G. Moyes: *Australian Cricket: A History* (Sydney, 1959), 152.

4

The Team

Cricket is traditionally a summer sport. Enthusiasts a century ago were not so restricted and Englishmen played in late October gales. In the Western District, cricket was played in June 1867, a period now sacred to football. A combined team from Pine Hill and Mullagh stations played Harrow club. The 'gigantic' Bullocky took the field for Harrow, apparently undaunted by his recent tour. Mullagh did not play for his station although Red Cap, Harry Rose and his brother (evidently King Cole of the subsequent English tour) helped that team to defeat Harrow by 88 runs. They also were playing cricket seriously in Edenhope during early August, despite the likelihood of frost and rain. The sickly Aboriginal team which returned three months earlier was reconstituted and members were practising regularly on the shores of Lake Wallace.

Unheralded and unnoticed by the press, a Sydney promoter arrived in the district and when his presence was reported in mid-August the team was already formed and a European tour was contemplated. Whether Charles Lawrence, Sydney cricket coach and hotelier, was accompanied by his two new Sydney business partners is difficult to establish. One of them, George Smith, had served terms as a Sydney alderman. From December 1857 to 1859 he represented the Macquarie Ward, followed by a term as alderman for the Fitzroy Ward until 1860. He became the manager of the English tour and, while there, possessed sufficient capital to purchase stallion bloodstock and ship his horses home. Smith's cousin, George W. Graham, an Elizabeth Street solicitor, was the silent partner who provided substantial capital, kept general accounts and frequently travelled with the team, although he remained in England after its departure for Australia.

William Hayman was the fourth investor. These speculators must be considered to have been just that — they expected high financial returns for their investment of capital and time. The time factor was considerable for all four men, but for Lawrence and Hayman it involved more than 18 months. Events established them as sincere men, who kept the interests of the Aborigines before them. They were fair employers and their organization proved remarkably effective. Lawrence, especially, also was a persuasive character. In the face of the previous disastrous and criticized tour, he convinced the Aborigines and the local pastoralists that this second tour was genuine. His recruiting drive was said to have enlisted 'the best of those who were left alive after the last tour and some other darkies'.

Cricket historians are indebted to Bill O'Reilly who appreciated the significance of finding Graham's ledger for the 1868 tour. He was given the book by an anonymous well-wisher in a Strathfield, NSW, pub in 1962. It is probably no coincidence that the Crossways pub is on the corner of the Hume Highway and Homebush Road, Sydney, because it was at 16 Homebush Street that Graham lived. However, O'Reilly was unable to glean any information about the history of the book between 1869, when the last entries were made, and the day when it came into his possession.[1]

The ledger contains a comprehensive and almost complete financial account of the tour. There is a statement of receipts and expenditure together with newspaper reports for each match (see Appendix V). Some accounts also include other incidental expenses. Unfortunately Graham failed to note the name and date of some press cuttings so it has not been possible to check them all. In addition to the match accounts there are two summary accounts — one giving Graham's transations before and during the tour, and the other relating to commissions earned and paid to E. F. Hingston of Liverpool, probably for printing and publicity for various matches. In assessing the overall financial result of the tour, the Hingston account can be ignored because all entries were included in Graham's general statement and the match accounts.

Graham's ledger entries establish that he eventually paid out more than £2200 to cover expenses for the tour, but what is relevant in this context are the details his entries provide of the preliminary preparations. Lawrence received £25 on 20 July 1867 'to proceed to Lake Wallace', and during August, Hayman was paid £301.16.6, followed by a further £201.8.0 in September.[2]

Lawrence took positive steps to identify with the team once he arrived at Lake Wallace, not the least of which was to endear his enterprise to the local press, with the result that his activities received sympathetic treatment. Given the earlier debacle it was an achievement to have it broadcast throughout the district that he was a man of good character, whose association with the project was 'sufficient guarantee . . . to the public that upon this occasion the whole affair was genuine'. With a nice sense of publicity, Lawrence requested the Melbourne Cricket Club to arrange a fixture during the Duke of Edinburgh's visit later in the year. The team practised hard and by early September it had played three games against scratch teams. These were followed by an advertisement in the *Hamilton Spectator*, issuing a challenge from Lawrence's XI, to all-comers in the Western District, whether teams of 16 or 18. Probably this was bravado, calculated to raise the morale of his men and publicize their existence.

A match played on 28 August, followed by two further challenge matches, probably guided Lawrence in his final selection of the team. His all-Aboriginal team comprised

Mullagh, Cuzens, Bullocky, Peter, Tarpot, Dick-a-Dick, Neddy (Jim Crow), S. Harry, Harry Rose and C. Rose (almost certainly King Cole, of the tour). The Edenhope club team also included the following Aborigines: Redcap, Sundown, Stock-keeper, Storekeeper and Gorman. In a morale boosting game, Lawrence's team won comfortably with a total of 174 to 47 runs by the opposition.

During his stay on the shores of Lake Wallace, Lawrence encouraged the Aborigines to practice their traditional skills with spear and boomerang. His encouragement included making supplies of these weapons and rehearsing games 'which pleased them very much and they soon became proficient and willing to do anything that I wanted them to learn'. The development of 'team spirit' was a matter which exercised Lawrence's mind. Perhaps his most important measure concerned dress. He designed an outlandish garb, with uniforms for both cricket and athletics, which possessed the dual advantages of giving pleasure and warmth to the wearers. Lawrence must have drawn upon his experience of the All-England XI tours, with their standardized shirts, sashes and hat bands. His cricketers may not have looked modish, but they were colourful. They took to the cricket field decked in white flannel trousers, military red shirts (a shirt-like blouse called a Garibaldi), with diagonal blue flannel sashes, blue elastic belts and neckties, white linen collars and beneath this finery were 'French merino undershirts'. The ensemble was completed with individually coloured peaked caps. For athletics, there were individually coloured caps and trunks, with long white tights worn beneath (described in one of the English papers as 'Oh–no–we–never–mention–'ems').

The coloured caps had been decided upon before the team left Edenhope, and not after the team's arrival in England as some writers have suggested. As befitted a European, Lawrence wore a white cap; why Red Cap was cast as the villain in a black cap is beyond explanation. Mullagh donned the red; Cuzens wore purple; Dick-a-Dick, yellow; Mosquito, dark blue; Peter, green; Jim Crow (Neddy), pink; Bullocky, chocolate; King Cole, magenta; Sundown, check; H. Rose, Victoria plaid; and Twopenny, McGregor plaid. However, by the time the team played in England some caps had changed heads and each cap bore an emblem of a silver boomerang and a bat, and players also wore a sash of their own colour to facilitate identification.[3]

The capacious wagon and its accompanying baggage wagon lumbered out of Edenhope on 16 September on the first stage of the team's English saga. It was apparently crammed with Lawrence, Hayman, a cook, a coachman, 12 Aboriginal cricketers and their gear. It was fortunate for the Aborigines that Lawrence, a temperate drinker, had replaced Wills. In deciding upon wagon transport, the management was in the van of progress. About this time, a nostalgic Harrow resident reported 'a new phase in our carriage accommodation this year. Bullock teams have well nigh passed away, and horse waggons have become their substitutes...It is a sign of advancing civilization, when these old colonial institutions are getting swept away'.[4]

Who were these Aborigines about to embark on this unusual mission, and where did they originate? There is considerable confusion on this subject in later commentaries and it is difficult to assemble authenticated detail. Fortunately, the alleged tribal names of most cricketers are preserved in a curious phonetic form in a page of a scorebook, partly reproduced in an English newspaper, and this provides some tenuous clues (see Appendix IV). However, all the Aborigines answered to European-given names, many of them derived from their station associations. Mullagh is the most obvious example; Cuzens, it was claimed, was named for a Balmoral storekeeper.

Despite beliefs to the contrary, it can be asserted that with two probable and one possible exception, both the 1866 and 1867 teams were recruited from western Victoria. They came

chiefly from the country stretching from Balmoral to Naracoorte, just across the South Australian border, and areas to
the north. At least, it can be claimed that they were domi-
ciled there before the cricketing vogue swept the area. Most
of the names become familiar to readers of *Hamilton Spectator* files after 1865. Twopenny was a newcomer in 1867 and,
as he later played cricket in Sydney and represented New
South Wales, it is possible that he was a recruit brought
down by Lawrence for coaching. On the other hand, he
returned to Victoria with the team in 1869, after its arrival in
Sydney from England. As already indicated, Charley
Dumas, a replacement for Harry Rose, who returned to the
Mount Talbot area from Geelong, almost certainly was recruited by Lawrence in New South Wales. It has been said
that Tarpot came from Bendigo, but in the context of this
attribution, it more likely represents a typographical error
for Benayeo station. In later life, Tarpot remained within the
region from which the team was recruited. Most significantly, a contemporary source stated that Tarpot was brother to
Jellico and Dick-a-Dick; another source claimed kinship between Dick-a-Dick and Jim Crow. 'Brother' in an Aboriginal
context is more likely to imply a less direct clan kinship, but
there is no reason to doubt some form of affiliation. Jellico
was the champion cricketer of Bringalbert, while Dick-a-
Dick has been termed 'King Richard' and a 'sub-chief' of his
tribe; whatever these European concepts actually meant in
regard to his tribal status, it implies that this was his territory. It is relevant to observe that although most of the
so-called tribal names listed in the scorebook and English
newspaper are probably only nicknames or poorly under-
stood renderings, all of them are in conformity with the
dialects of the area. They have nothing in common with the
languages of the adjoining South Australian Jaralde group,
or other non-Victorian languages. Dick-a-Dick's name possibly was authentic: 'jangan-djina-njug' means 'walking feet'.

It is concluded that all but two team members claimed the

southern Wimmera region as traditional territory. They mostly were affiliated with the Madimadi and Wutjubaluk 'tribes', which more correctly are described as language or dialect groupings. In traditional times they normally would have lived in bands; depending upon seasonal conditions, these bands might number from 20 to 100 individuals. Such bands often occupied territorial units approximating in area to that of many European stations, but they congregated occasionally for social and ceremonial reasons into groups numbering a few hundred. At such meetings, gifts and marriage partners were exchanged between bands, thereby establishing kinship networks and mutual obligations. In this manner, cricketers descended from related females might be described as brothers. During their long absence from traditional places, the team members must have found this social bonding a consolation in unfamiliar surroundings.[5]

The ages of team members are uncertain. They were all men of full Aboriginal descent and most of them were born before pastoral occupation began. Mullagh, the best known of all Western District Aborigines, was believed to have been born around 1845. At the inquest upon his death, Watty was recorded as 33 years old; King Cole was reported to be 30 at the time of his death in 1868. Mission officials later estimated that Tarpot was born in 1843, Harry Rose around 1847, Cuzens in 1845 and Tiger in 1836. From their photographs, a few might be judged in their late teens, although the majority looked older. Their luxuriant whiskers render guessing hazardous. When the group was photographed with Wills (Plate 21), he was about 32; most of his team look more youthful than he.

There are vital statistics available for a few of the men. Cowell, who played with Mullagh in 1865, described him as being about 5 ft 10 in (178 cm) tall. An interested sports writer measured three of them in England, although with difficulty, as they would not permit him to take all the measurements which he sought. He confirmed what other writers observed, that Dick-a-Dick was 'a strong muscular man', 5 ft 8½ in (174 cm) tall; Charley Dumas was 5 ft 10 in (178 cm), while Cuzens was a tiny person, only 5ft 1 in (155 cm) tall and very small-boned. On the other hand, Bullocky always was described as a burly, large man.[6]

The fullest appraisal of the team was provided by Charles Box, an English writer on cricket, remarkable for its sympathetic treatment:[7]

> The colour of skin was certainly not black, but rather a sooty brown; the hair a jet black, in every instance, and curly, but not so harsh or stiff in the curl as the African negro; in form, straight and upright, rather slight limbed, with small hands and feet, tolerably broad shoulders, and a sinking of the chest indicative of weak lungs. Their faces varied considerably in formation, especially in the nose, with higher foreheads than the negro; and, notwithstanding an evident training of the whiskers and moustache, thereby conveying a fierce military aspect, there was, generally speaking, an amount of docility somewhat prepossessing; eyes large and full with a soft expression, and a physiogamy, taken altogether, by no means unintellectual . . .it was observed that in all of them there was a manly and dignified bearing.

Contrast that description with the contemptuous and racist perception of the celebrated novelist Anthony Trollope.[8] As a tourist and columnist in Australia about this time, he dismissed comparable men with the observation: 'To my eyes the deportment of the dignified aboriginal is that of a sapient monkey imitating the gait and manners of a do-nothing white dandy.'

When the expedition arrived at Warrnambool, an obliging photographer there, P. Dawson, photographed the members individually, taking much trouble over the task, although he charged for his costs only. Perhaps his generosity explains why his business fell into financial straits shortly afterwards.

Assembled and published by H. de Gruchy and Company, Melbourne, this group of 16 photographs is a cricketing classic, a memorable study in Victoriana and a document of considerable ethnographic interest (Plate 24).

Only five of the 14 Aborigines wore their cricket dress or adopted cricketing poses, and one of them (Rose) did not sail to England. It is perhaps significant that the others — Mullagh, Cuzens, Red Cap and Bullocky — were the backbone of the team in England. It is as though the other members were selected for different talents in the full knowledge that they were not true cricketers. They are dressed in their athletics outfit and posed with an interesting and representative collection of western Victorian wooden offensive and defensive weapons. They demonstrated the use of them all on their English tour, including spears and spear throwers, boomerangs, fighting clubs and parrying shields. The Europeans in the group are an interesting trio. Lawrence sports his white cap, looking dapper and alert, while Smith is seated at a desk, every inch a solid, portly executive. Hayman is a caricature of Victorian cricket, as he stands gazing sternly ahead, erect but with his legs crossed, wearing a tall top hat, dress coat and luxuriant side whiskers, his bat tucked under an arm, handle grasped in most unorthodox fashion.

Although it seems probable that the team was photographed frequently in England, few examples have been traced. W. B. Tegetmeier, the amateur ethnologist who measured Dumas, Cuzens and Dick-a-Dick, also arranged for them to be photographed. The portrait of the latter conveyed, he thought, his 'stern determination', reminiscent of Blondin; the 'wonderful' portrait of Dumas was sharp, despite the dullness of the day requiring him to remain rigid for more than 80 seconds.

Covered wagons in 1867 were making history on American prairies, sometimes facing attack from the indigenous inhabitants. By contrast, the American wagon which lumbered along the muddy track towards Harrow on a wet spring day was loaded with indigenous Australians (near Warrnambool they were almost attacked by Europeans on horseback, but Lawrence and his men fired first and they rode off). Four horsepower proved insufficient and they bogged. Caught in a thunderstorm, the team managed to construct a brush shelter and light a fire, waiting through a cold night until morning to unload the vehicle and manhandle it out of the mud. The next evening was more enjoyable, with grilled chops and billy tea, as they sat and joked around the fire. They passed through Harrow on the third morning and camped that night beside a waterhole near Coleraine. Another day's journey brought them to the comfort of a Hamilton hotel. Celebrities now, they were feted at dinner by all sportsmen, but lack of time made them decline an invitation to play the new-fangled football game which Tom Wills had introduced a few years previously.

Bush life was proving too tiring for Lawrence, who stayed behind to rest a day in the hotel, while Hayman went on with the team. Lawrence soon rejoined them by travelling in a buggy. Near disaster followed on the next day. Diminutive Cuzens was driving the wagon when its wheels struck rocks and he overbalanced, landing on his head, while the horses bolted. Fortunately, his jolting caused nothing worse than a headache.

After eight adventurous days on the road they reached Warrnambool, where they rested a week before their morale-boosting appearance on the Warrnambool ground. They scored 140 and then twice dismissed the local XVI for totals of 19 and 24. Mullagh, who scored 48 not out, also took 10 wickets in the first innings, while a total of 18 batsmen failed to score for Warrnambool. During the journey Dick-a-Dick and Cuzens had shown deep interest in simple stories which Lawrence told them about the life of Christ and the elements of Christianity. When he was aged about 86, by which time punctuation seemed unimportant, Lawrence started his memoirs, which he never finished. Their simple questions remained in his mind as he recalled that on the following Sunday nine Aborigines accompanied him to the Church of England:

> I took them all to church as I had promised they seemed to like it and was [sic] very attentive and when the collection plate was presented they gave a little help. When they came out I asked them how they liked it they replied this way. Music very nice and him talk a lot and get a lot of money. I said and what do you think he does with it. Keep it don't he I said no but gives it to the poor people they were quite astounded and said does he then. Well when we go to church again I will always put my money in the plate which I am pleased to say they did.

Lawrence found that such decorum was not habitual. One night one of the team entered his Warrnambool hotel room after his mates were in bed. It was a large dormitory with a chandelier in the centre, which could be pulled up or down. As he wanted to light his pipe, he 'made a jump and clinging to the chandelier brought it down with a crash...the kerosene ignited the whole room'. Fortunately, the fire was soon extinguished, although considerable damage resulted.

On the road again, a few days later they arrived in Mortlake. Rain interrupted the game there and the pitch was so wet that the ball simply stuck firmly in the mud. The match was abandoned after the home team made 40 and the Aborigines had lost 5 wickets for 25 runs. They resumed their laborious trek to Geelong. From there it was intended to take the team to Ballarat, Castlemaine, Bendigo and Melbourne, before moving on to Sydney.[9]

Even well-planned enterprises encounter difficulties; Lawrence had already overcome many, but he was about to face a real crisis. Back in Edenhope on 15 August, Mounted Constable Kennedy raised the question of the cricketers with his superior in Portland. Since Lawrence had mustered them on the shores of Lake Wallace, he reported, 'the majority of them have been drunk', and were so disorderly that three of them were currently in the lock-up. In a thoughtful statement, Kennedy requested that the Central Board for the Protection of the Aborigines be asked to intervene. He stressed the misfortunes of the earlier tour and the fact that several of the new team suffered from chest ailments, but he agreed that the Aborigines had been invited (at least nominally) to join the party and that their decisions had been arrived at freely. He also knew from experience, however, 'what a potent reasoner a glass of grog is with a blackfellow'. What action Lawrence and Hayman, manager once again, had taken to prevent this roistering is unknown. The subsequent behaviour of the team is sufficient proof that the drink problem was controlled, if not countered. Perhaps the management set a better example and they were continually on hand. The evident denial of leisure time during their marathon Australian and English tours is a possible contributing factor to Aboriginal sobriety.

Kennedy's report, together with an indignant letter from Dr Molloy of Balmoral, reached the central board's secretary, Brough Smyth, early in October. Molloy's letter was also published in Melbourne newspapers. At its meeting on 11 October the board resolved 'to appeal to the Chief Secretary and Attorney-General for aid in preventing the sending of aboriginal cricketers to England and using them for profit in neighbouring colonies'; and put a note in Melbourne newspapers. Their appeal evoked no response, presumably for the same reasons that their February moves failed — there was no legal basis for intervention.

Brough Smyth's only recourse was to appeal to public opinion. In its press campaign the board made much of Molloy's humanitarian letter, in which he claimed that change of climate and alcohol would prove fatal to the team. Smyth concluded with a rather melodramatic appeal to 'all right-minded persons in putting an end to the heartless proceedings of the speculators who unscrupulously endanger the lives of the blacks for the sake of sordid gain...It is imagined it is but needful to place the matter fairly before a humane public to ensure the hearty opposition to...all schemes of every right minded man'.

The board members are to be praised for their indignation and prompt action, in light of the previous tour which had fulfilled their worst prognostications. However, 'right minded' editors and readers were rare. The *Age* and *Argus* quoted Smyth's letter in full, but offered no comment. No readers wrote to the editors, or at least their letters were unpublished; instead, cricket followers were exercising their minds and pens on the iniquitous MCC, whose committee resolved to erect a seven-foot-high fence at their ground. An egalitarian society regarded such exclusive behaviour as snobbery.[10]

The keynote of Molloy's letter had been that the players would be 'used up' by their sponsors. The *Age* used this theme to turn the argument against the board's appeal, thereby revealing its lack of sympathy for that body's stand. It published a long account of the Aboriginal match at Geelong and contrasted the situation with their appearance there in January. It is a tribute to Lawrence's firm control, even if the imagery is unduly colourful.

A marked improvement in their bearing is noticeable, and as they sat at table, mixed indiscriminately with the members of the club...their conversation and lively manners were sufficient to convince those who had met them before that if they are being 'used up', there is nothing perceptible of it either in their bodily or mental calibre; but on the contrary, they appear as temperate as anchorites, as jolly as sandboys and as supple as deer.

The weather continued quite unsuitable for cricket, so this Geelong match was drawn, with the Corio club leading the Aborigines on the first innings. On this occasion, T. W.

Wills played for Corio against the Aborigines, evidently un-happy that he had not been involved in this tour. Wills quickly captured four Aboriginal wickets, but Lawrence struck back by bowling him leg before wicket for 6 runs.

Public apathy over the team's fate notwithstanding, Law-rence and his associates must have feared the loss of their investment. Although George Smith had written to the Mel-bourne Cricket Club optimistically requesting a fixture dur-ing the November visit of the Duke of Edinburgh, that club referred the request to its Match and Ground Committee in September and there is no record of further action. At this time the committee had controversial matters of ground development before it. Unless there was some verbal and unrecorded reply, this failure to respond contrasted with its attitude earlier in the year. It must have concerned the team's management. Was the MCC influenced by the Board for the Protection of the Aborigines' appeal to prevent the tour? Was T. W. Wills a negative influence in this matter? Probably not, as he held no position on the committee. Although Wills was said to have been unaware of Lawrence's initiative until he learned that the team had left Lake Wal-lace, this claim seems unlikely, in view of Lawrence's close involvement with the later stages of the previous abortive Sydney tour. Besides, would Wills have been available for such a prolonged overseas tour as was proposed? He had been reappointed recently as cricket tutor at the Melbourne ground and he was involved with football during the winter. During his active career, he played more than 210 games of football, mostly with Melbourne and Geelong, and was one of the stars of the new game, the rules of which he was partly responsible for. It was claimed by his sympathetic supporter 'Longstop', W. J. Hammersley, the *Australasian*'s cricket writer, that he had been offended by being excluded from further involvement with the Aborigines. In September, Wills had written to 'Longstop' complaining of Lawrence's action. From the tone of that letter, 'Longstop' deduced that 'he is a little hurt at being overthrown in the matter' of coaching the Aborigines. He used his column to observe that 'we have had...quite enough of Aboriginal cricket for some time to come', and urged the MCC not to make their ground available to them. He added that credit for coaching the Aborigines still remained with Wills. Unfortunately, the folklore about this tour still honours Wills, rather than Tom Hamilton and friends, or Lawrence.

This issue of coaching merits clarification. Wills was a Victorian hero and remains an immortal in the annals of football and cricket, but his role with this team was more limited. For possibly two seasons before his involvement, the Aborigines had been encouraged and tutored by Hamilton, Edgar, Hayman and others. Wills first met the team late in November 1866. Before the match started in Melbourne on 26 December, he had a maximum period of three weeks in which to coach, because the journey to Melbourne must have taken several days. Between January and early May 1867, Wills captained the team and did much to hold it together with his batting and bowling. However, interruptions due to bad weather, team illnesses, legal disputes and shortage of funds must have restricted coaching hours. Lawrence spent at least as much time coaching at Lake Wallace as Wills had done. As later chapters illustrate, he travelled continuously with the team for more than 16 months, captaining it on all Australian engagements and leading the team on to English fields for 40 of its 47 matches.

It was unwise to tarry in the colony. The return match at Geelong on 18–19 October was their last in Victoria. It was drawn, although wagers of 10 to 1 on an Aboriginal victory had been accepted. The Aborigines scored 64 and 73, while Corio made 37 and was four wickets for 29 in its second innings, so the Aborigines were unlucky that rain intervened! There were 1000 spectators in attendance at the athletics, to see 60 cricket balls hurled at a dodging Dick-a-Dick without any hitting his body.

Life off the cricket field also was not without incident and humour. On their first night in Geelong, a weary Lawrence went to bed early, leaving the team to stroll around town. They returned later to the hotel and then sat drinking in one of their rooms. The publican, who crept to the door to see what was happening, became so terrified by what he heard that he rushed to wake up Lawrence. 'They are going to kill me and then set fire to the house,' he told Lawrence, 'please therefore at once send for the police.' Lawrence told him to wait: 'I immediately went to the blacks to hear their trouble they laughed and said we saw him list[en]ing and thought we would frighten him it was only for fun and we are sorry...I called him in and they said they would not be bad Blackfellows again if he would forgive them which he did and gave them all a drink and they parted good friends...next day the landlord was dancing with them and gave them anything they wanted.'

On another evening, some men chatted with Dick-a-Dick who 'being the greatest swell and more intelligent was asked to have a walk round the town'. He arrived back at the hotel proudly bearing a new belltopper hat, complete with hat-box and an invitation to meet the donor's family in the morning. In the genteel surroundings in which he was presented to the ladies on the next day, Dick-a-Dick nervously stood up, leaving his new hat on the chair. The man who faced speeding cricket balls with such aplomb then sat down, crushing his hat. Exit hat, but the ladies invited Dick-a-Dick to return. From such fleeting anecdotes, and despite their jocular 'innocents abroad' theme, the team appears as a boyish, lively group of individuals with character. It is evident that, in retrospect, Lawrence remembered the amiable and curious Dick-a-Dick with real affection.[11]

Although it was announced that the team would play in Bendigo on 2 November, before moving to Ballarat and Castlemaine, this was bluff. The ruse of the Queenscliff fishing holiday and the unscheduled exit on the *Rangatira* off

Port Phillip Heads was a shrewd but contemptuous gesture. Perhaps Lawrence appreciated public sentiment better than did the central board. Sympathy lay unreservedly with Captain Lawrence and his smuggled cargo. 'The black cricketers have been too many for the Board', was all the *Argus* had to offer; 'check-mated by the speculators' was the *Age* observation on the board's action. The *Australasian* supported the smugglers and adapted a *Sydney Morning Herald* item to this end. Another Sydney paper scorned the board's stand: 'they endeavoured to prevent the team from leaving, but Messrs Hayman and Lawrence were too smart for them'. Lawrence's own account of the dramatic events is cryptic: 'a notice appeared in a Melbourne newspaper that the Blacks protection Society was urging upon the Government to prevent the Blacks...leaving the country therefore the Matches that had been arranged in Victoria had to be abandoned and we left for New South Wales.'

Around this stirring period, the Edenhope squatter J. P. Hayman chanced to visit Melbourne. He was astonished to find his nephew, William, staying at his regular lodging, a Flinders Street hotel, the Port Phillip Club. In a letter to his wife, he commented that 'the blacks have been shipped off to Sydney as the Black protectors stated they would do their best to prevent their going so they gave them the slip'. William must have been there to arrange their passage to Sydney and he may have collected the team photographic montage from H. de Gruchy and Company. Hayman also reported that William was awaiting the arrival of two Aboriginal replacements for three team members who had been sent home from Geelong (in fact, probably only Harry Rose actually departed). Those expected were Tarpot and Billy Officer, although Tiger probably substituted for the latter. As William was leaving for Sydney on 29 October, he must have devised some further ruse for transporting this duo without attracting attention.[12]

Team morale was high after its disembarkation in Sydney.

The Aborigines played their first match at Wollongong on 6 and 7 November and won by eight wickets. Illawarra scored 27 and 102, but the Aborigines made 86 and two wickets for 45. The usual athletic sports were greeted with interest, although the spectators caused problems similar to the unruly crowding at the first athletics meeting there in April. Dick-a-Dick and Cuzens ran a fine race, but neither could stop before crashing into the spectators. Cuzens sent a baby spinning from the arms of its mother and he himself lay 'stunned' for some hours. Dick-a-Dick collided with a horse, knocking horse and rider to the ground. Fortunately, nobody was seriously injured.

The team continued to play a good standard of cricket and even to lift their performance. On 11 and 12 November they were victorious at West Maitland and went on to defeat the Singleton team by 10 wickets in a one-day match. At Newcastle, on 15 and 16 November, they won by nine wickets. In a match against a strong team at the Albert Ground, however, they lost by 15 runs. On Boxing Day they also lost to the Bathurst club. The team was based at Manly Beach, guests of Lawrence's Pier Hotel, on the Esplanade. At this time a well-wisher commented on the fact that they received religious instruction, attended church regularly and were well spoken, temperate and well dressed.

On 4 and 5 February the Duke of Edinburgh twice drove his team of four greys to the Albert Ground to witness the Aborigines play their final Australian match. It was against an Army and Navy team, which included William Caffyn. Four thousand spectators saw the home team dismissed for 64, Cuzens taking 8 wickets for 23 runs. The Aborigines scored 237, of which Cuzens compiled 86, Mullagh 56 and Bullocky 39. Cuzens ran 10 fours in his attacking innings. The match ended in a draw, when Army and Navy were 2 wickets down for 51. Against this opposition, Caffyn prudently did not offer to challenge them single-handed as he had done the previous season. On the second day, 9000 had entered the ground, perhaps in response to a large advertisement in the *Sydney Morning Herald*. After the match, there was an athletics meeting, and Mullagh cleared 5 feet 7 inches in the high jump, possibly his best effort. An exhibition of Aboriginal prowess followed, the feature attraction of which was a mock battle, six men to a side. They appeared in a new costume which thrilled the onlookers. It comprised a 'black closely fitting underdress, a doublet of oppossum skins, and a parti-coloured headdress, turned up with a broad band of cabbage-tree plait', and a crest of lyre-bird plumage. Around this same time real-life drama was being staged. Bushranger Thunderbolt held up the northern mail coach and the Duke of Edinburgh was wounded in Sydney by a would-be assassin.

The first Australian cricket team to tour England sailed from Sydney on 8 February. It was appropriate that this team from the heart of Victoria's sheep pastures chose to voyage on the *Parramatta*, a vessel laden with wool (Plate 24A). Unlucky Tarpot was too ill to sail and left the ship before its departure. Despite his disabilities, however, he was destined to outlive his more travelled team-mates. Because Tarpot had married just before the team left Edenhope in September, he had not journeyed in the wagon. He set out independently with his wife and only joined them later. Harry Rose, of the Victoria plaid cap, had left the party at Geelong, and perhaps Twopenny and Jim Crow were fortunate to be on board, because the *Age* had reported that they also were returning home with Rose.[13]

Accompanying the Aborigines on their long tour were Lawrence, Hayman, Smith and Graham. It was an efficient combination. Lawrence, then in his 40th year, was a conscientious and resourceful captain; Smith and Graham were equipped to arrange and finance the complex tour. Hayman, who is credited by commentators with managing the team, possibly was concerned more directly with Aboriginal welfare and care of the team's gear. His long association with them, his sincerity and enthusiasm for their cause (he apparently acted as scorer for most English games), and the fact that he was their only direct link with their tribal lands, must have placed him in a position of trust as adviser and intermediary. Hayman did not sail with the team, as he went on ahead by the previous ship to make arrangements about accommodation and training. The efficient planning of the tour is evident, matches being arranged in many counties and the team always took the field on the scheduled day. Although this was the age of Victorian technological progress, travel within England posed problems of timetable, connections and bad roads. Richard Daft, the Nottingham professional, mentioned some of the transport problems of the itinerant cricketer in his discursive memoirs. Given conditions such as these, it is evident that the Aborigines were in capable administrative hands.[14]

The *Warrnambool Examiner*, on 1 October 1867, had pictured the team 'like a happy travelling family'. While the team lodged at Warrnambool's Victoria Hotel, and on their long wagon trek, members had employed their leisure time in hunting and native dancing. They also showed proficiency at dancing waltzes and polkas, and played billiards, whist and écarté. With this combination of native and European attainments they whiled away their time aboard ship. They would have proved an asset to the ship's entertainment officer.

Aboard the *Parramatta*, the Aborigines were given a large cabin, situated between the first and second class areas. The ship's master, Captain Williams, obviously felt well disposed towards the men. He and Lawrence took care to ensure that they overcame any fear of the sea, at the same time instructing them in a very simple Christianity. This education continued the stories told to Dick-a-Dick and Cuzens round the camp fire while on the track. Evidently Captain Williams joined Lawrence and the team for evening prayers. Lawrence recorded events in his usual, unpunctuated prose:

They very soon lost all fear of the sea voyage as they heard the captain pray and said to me does he know Jesus Christ and the little pickaninny you used to tell us about that we saw in the picture and Dick-a-Dick said they kill him. I told them that Jesus was in heaven now and that the captain prayed to him that we should all arrive safely in England nothing seemed now to trouble them for they thought the captain was so good that the ship would never sink I took a good supply of copy books and endeavoured to teach them to write and read I gave them lessons every morning but this did not last long for they soon tired and amused themselves in drawing trees birds and all kinds of animals and anything they could think of Drafts and cards they liked and to play with the children and to get pieces of wood from the carpenter and to make needles and lots of other little things for the ladies one gave them a [tatting] shuttle to see if they could make one which they did they therefore became great favourites with the ladies and their children always wanted to be with the Blacks who were in good health.

When the vessel arrived off the English coast, the Aborigines became doubly upset. News came aboard that the Duke of Edinburgh had been shot and wounded in Sydney, soon after watching the Aboriginal cricketers. They decided that they would perform their games before the duke in England as a welcome for him. A much more traumatic experience followed when they heard that the captain was to leave the ship for the pilot to take command. They remained disturbed until he took positive action:

After breakfast the captain said he would like to have the Blacks together in their cabin to bid them goodbye...but before doing so he wanted to say a few words to them as he was afraid they might be led astray in England he therefore said now Boys I have to thank you for your good behaviour during this passage and to give you a little

advice as you will meet with as many thieves and vaga-
bonds as hairs on your head and they will tell you that you
are very [clever] and then ask you to have some drink and
then rob you so don't have anything to do with them but
do just what Mr Lawrence wishes you to do...he also
spoke very kindly to them shook hands and bid them
goodbye. They cried a good deal when he left, two days
later we arrived at [Gravesend].

William Hayman was there to greet them and take them to
their base which he had arranged at Town Malling, in Kent
(now West Malling). With remarkably fortunate timing, the
Surrey Cricket Club was holding its annual dinner that
night, near London Bridge. Lawrence therefore remained
aboard and continued on to London, where he attended the
dinner. When he arrived next day at Town Malling, he
found his team 'in good spirits and anxious to play, they all
gained in weight on the voyage'.

After a voyage of three months, therefore, the Aborigines
arrived at their destination. They had received greater solicitude than did those thousands of Irish migrants who made
the outward voyage during the decade. It was a unified team,
devoted to their captain, and not an assemblage of individualistic tribesmen, which disembarked in England.[15]

NOTES

[1] The recruitment of the new team and winter cricket are inferred from
H.S., 12 June, 14, 28, 31 August, 4, 11, 18 September 1867. G. W.
Graham lived at 16 Homebush Street, Homebush. In a letter to *Sporting
Life* on 14 January 1869, he stated that Smith was his cousin (Graham,
Accounts, 122). Bill O'Reilly described the circumstances of the accounts
ledger in a letter to Mulvaney on 3 May 1982; a copy of this letter is in
the MCC archives.

[2] The financial statements refer to Graham's ledger, p 269. Details
concerning George Smith were supplied by the Protocol Officer, Town
Hall, Sydney.

[3] The events prior to departure from Edenhope are based upon *H.S.*,

11, 18 September 1867, *Aust.*, 21 September 1867; the trial game, *H.S.*, 28 August 1867. Lawrence's comment: Lawrence MS 1, p 52. The team uniforms and colours are described in *Aust.*, 5 October 1867, 428; *The Times*, 26 May 1868. The changes in dress by the first English fixture were that Lawrence appeared capless and Cuzens wore his white cap. Mullagh changed to dark blue; Jim Crow brown; Tiger pink; C. Dumas light blue; Bullocky maroon; Twopenny drab. The silver emblem is referred to in *Maidstone Journal*, June 1868.

4 The journey to Warrnambool: *Aust.*, 5 October 1867, 428; the nostalgic observer, *H.S.*, 16 October 1867. Lawrence's own account, MS 1, 53–9.

5 Who were the Aborigines? Tarpot was said to come from Bendigo in *Kowree Advocate* (Edenhope), 24 March 1959; *Aust.*, 16 February 1867, 203 also gives Bendigo, but the context is more probably Benayeo. His relationship to Dick-a-Dick, *Aust.*, 11 May 1867. Status of Dick-a-Dick: F. K. McKenzie, in *Back to Bill's Gully and Yanipy*, souvenir booklet (Kaniva, 1939), 3; his relationship to Jim Crow: Dr Luise Hercus, taped interview with Jack Long, Point Pearce, 10 May 1971 (Hercus Tapie 3g2, side B). For advice on linguistic matters, we are indebted to Dr Hercus, who has been responsible for documenting many Victorian languages.

6 Aboriginal photographs: P. Dawson, letter in *H.S.*, 10 February 1869; *Warrnambool Examiner*, 8 October 1867. The English photographs and measurements: letters by W. B. Tegetmeier in *The Field* (Graham, Accounts, 335). Description of Mullagh by A. A. Cowell, *H.S.*, 27 August 1891, 3.

7 C. Box, *The English Game of Cricket* (London, 1877), 324.

8 A. Trollope, *Australia and New Zealand* (Melbourne, 1976), 63.

9 The Warrnambool trek: largely based upon Lawrence MS 1, 52–60; the hotel fire, Lawrence MS 2, 2: MS 1 consists of 68 handwritten pages of ruled exercise book, MS 2 is 3 loose sheets; MS 3 is 7 pages of notebook, all owned by Mr I. Friend. Other sources, *H.S.*, October 1867; Mortlake and beyond, *H.S.*, 12, 19 October 1867. Church attendance: *Warrnambool Examiner*, 1 October 1867.

10 Board intervention: Chief Secretary's papers: Letters inwards, 14 October 1867, no 210514 (State Library of Victoria, Archives). Molloy's letter: *Age* and *Argus*, 17 October 1867; Board's resolution: Minutes of the Central Board Appointed to Watch Over the Interests of the Aborigines, bound vol 1, folio, 11 October 1867. Smyth's letter: *Age* and *Argus*, 17 October 1867.

11 The Geelong incidents: Lawrence MS 1, 61 and MS 2: *Age*, 19 October 1867; Wills: *Aust.*, 14 September 1867, 332. MCC Annual Report 1867, 36, 43.

[12] The great escape: *Argus* and *Age*, 24 October 1867; *Aust.*, 16 November 1867; *S.M.H.*, 2 November 1867; *Illustrated Sydney News*, 16 November 1867, 262; Lawrence MS 1, 61. Hayman in Melbourne: J. P. Hayman to his wife, 28 October 1867 — copy courtesy Sir Peter Hayman.

[13] Illawarra: A. P. Fleming, *The International Aboriginal Cricketers v Illawarra* (Wollongong, 1968); other NSW matches: *H.S.*, 4 December 1867; *Aust.*, 16 November 1867; Army and Navy match: J. Milner and O. Brierley, *Cruise of H.M.S. Galatea* (London, 1869), 374; players reported returning home: *Age*, 24 October 1867.

[14] English transport: A. Daft, *Kings of Cricket* (Bristol [1893]), 210.

[15] The voyage was described by Lawrence MS 1, 62–6.

5

'Stalwart Men'

'Nothing of interest comes from Australia except gold nuggets and black cricketers,' quipped the London *Daily Telegraph* after the wool clipper *Parramatta* berthed at Gravesend on 13 May 1868 and the team began a brief training round at West Malling ground, Kent. It was 81 years to the day since the First Fleet sailed from Gravesend under Arthur Phillip to undertake the European occupation of Australia. This first Australian tour of England was a memorable one for the record books.

One record is certain to remain unsurpassed and that is the team's endurance marathon. Despite their meagre number, which was reduced to a mere 11 fit players during the tour, between their first match at the Oval on 25 May and their last engagement on the same ground on 15 to 17 October, the players were in the field 99 days out of a possible 126 (Sunday excluded); and they ranged almost as widely over the counties as is the practice of modern cricket tourists. Their 47 matches were played in 40 centres, across 15 counties (Figure E). Some team members even participated in a sports meeting at Plymouth at the conclusion of the tour. Considering that Australian Aborigines habitually have been criticized for rarely maintaining sustained application to a single task over a prolonged period, this was an outstanding refutation, certainly deserving the title 'Stalwart Men'.

The changing society of industrial Britain and an accompanying rise in the demand for spectator sports are reflected in the team's commercial circuit. The newer industrial centres were the focus of most matches. These venues were a response to the entertainment needs of the many non-participatory urban workers with from sixpence to half a crown for gate money.

Of the 47 fixtures, 10 were played in the general London region, 11 in the south-eastern counties and three in East Anglia, while 21 games were played in the Midlands and the north. The fixture at Swansea was the only engagement west of Reading, thereby ignoring the claims of the more rural western county towns, despite their later importance in the county championship competition. Such were the demands upon the players that 11 matches were staged during September and six in October, surely the most unseasonal international fixures in the history of the game.

Playing conditions more rigorous than those faced by modern touring sides also imposed difficulties and added strain. While matches normally lasted only two days, there were more of them, which added to the time spent travelling, often in uncomfortable vehicles and delays were prolonged while waiting for transport connections. The hours of play were longer also than at present. Play began at 11 a.m. or noon and usually continued until 7 p.m. or later. The addition of sporting exhibitions to the Aborigines' programme must have involved even longer hours. There were no tea breaks and the only interval was for lunch, a 35-minute period at some time between 2 and 3 p.m. Most grounds did not provide special catering facilities for the players who had to take their chance with the crowd which thronged refreshment tents. If he was lucky, a player emerged with beer and sandwiches. A colourful impression of catering arrangements back in Australia is provided by the print of the first All-England XI match at the Melbourne Cricket Ground on New Year's Day 1862 (Plate 4). At least seven refreshment tents fill the side foreground of the picture.

King Cole died of tuberculosis, probably accelerated by pneumonia, in Guy's Hospital, London, on 24 June. He was buried in the Victoria Park cemetery, London. Even in his Warrnambool picture his physique appeared slight. Sundown, who played in only two matches and compiled a single run, was ailing, and he was sent home with Jim Crow in August. This drain upon team reserves placed a tremendous burden on the shoulders of the able men. A testimony to the husbandry of human resources by the management is the performance of the remaining 11 Aborigines. Red Cap and Tiger played in all 47 matches, Cuzens in 46, Dick-a-Dick and Mullagh in 45. Lawrence and three others appeared on 40 or more occasions. It is hardly surprising, and relevant to any assessment of playing standards, that at the end of their tour a sympathetic sports writer observed in the men 'an amount of fatigue that now seems almost incredible'.[1]

West Malling was chosen as the base for the team's operations because of William Hayman's family connections. Indeed, his kinship network, together with Charles Lawrence's social links with the Surrey Cricket Club, explain many otherwise unconnected episodes of the tour. The Hayman family originated in Devon but had dispersed. While one of William's uncles pastured sheep at Lake Wallace, another lived in West Malling, less than 10 kilometres west of Maidstone. Most fortunately, he was married to a sister of a Kentish cricketing celebrity, William South Norton (1831–1916), who was then a vigorous man of 37. A former captain of the Kent County Cricket Club, he was still a player and its honorary secretary. As preceding years had witnessed rivalry between Kentish towns pressing claims for the location of the county cricket headquarters, it was alleged by the press that Norton was pushing the case for West Malling. Whatever the truth of the matter, the Aboriginal visit certainly attracted popular attention to its playing field.

Consequently, when Hayman took an early passage to England, with Graham's money drafts in his wallet, it is hardly surprising that his destination was West Malling. Norton's qualifications extended into professional management. In 1859 he had been president of Tom Sherman's New All-England XI, one of the professional teams competing for the popular circuit. It probably was only coincidence, but Lawrence and Sherman were schoolboy friends and played their first important match together when aged 14. It was an occasion when both drank too much sherry and failed dismally as cricketers. Lawrence considered that Sherman was one of the truly great English cricketers.

Norton's advice to Hayman evidently was positive. Hayman contracted with another administrator, E. P. Hingston, to arrange a schedule of grounds, to prepare publicity and to settle other administrative details. For his services throughout the tour, Hingston received five per cent of the team profits from each fixture. It was a good business arrangement, provided only that matches proved profitable. The co-operation of Norton may explain why the second and third fixtures of the tour were held on Kentish grounds. He played against the Aborigines in both the Maidstone and the Gravesend matches. His association with the team became so close that, when Lawrence was unavailable for the 10th match, the Aborigines began their battle at Hastings on 22 June, under Norton's leadership.[2]

Many years later, Norton recalled the dramatic arrival of the colonials, when Hayman escorted them from the ship to his West Malling home:

> I had no notice of the exact time I was to expect them, so when they all walked one morning into my house after breakfast they caused a good deal of excitement and curiousity. They had a little refreshment, and my two young daughters were brought into the room to inspect the blackies. The little ones were not at all frightened.

Surrey club connections proved equally important to the successful opening of the tour. The Aborigines played their first match at the Oval in a blaze of publicity. This newly opened ground was the triumph of the genial Surrey club secretary, William Burrup. It was Burrup who had assisted the departure of Stephenson's team to Australia in 1861. Lawrence felt indebted to him at that time, for the 'immense lot of trouble for our welfare', because Burrup had arranged life insurance for him and travelled to Liverpool to farewell the team on the *Great Britain*. They had been farewelled previously at a dinner, arranged by Burrup, at the Caesar family's Bridgehouse Hotel, London Bridge. By a happy chance, on the day Lawrence arrived back in London in 1868, he was able to attend the Surrey Club annual dinner at the same hotel, also organized by Burrup. Circumstances were therefore ideal for pressing the Surrey Club into service, as he renewed contact with many of the 100 guests. Actually, the surviving rudimentary minute book of the Surrey County Cricket Club fails to mention the Aboriginal team, so the personal role of Burrup in arranging the Oval fixtures seems likely.

The Surrey Club supplied one of its ground staff to accompany the Aboriginal tour as occasional relief player and umpire. William Shepherd (1841–1919) was a Kennington man who played for Surrey in 1864, but failed to keep his place. He represented the Aborigines on seven occasions, once as captain, but with very moderate success. To judge from his reminiscences, however, Shepherd enjoyed his association with the players (Plate 26).

Another Surrey player stood as umpire at the Oval. His name, Julius Caesar, seemed as much out of character on the cricket field as those of the visiting players. Caesar had toured Australia with Parr's XI and his characteristics were likely to prove popular in the Aboriginal camp. He was described by a team-mate as 'one of the liveliest members of our team, and a fast and big hitter'. As Caesar, who was a member of the Godalming Club, received 20 per cent of gate proceeds from their second last match at Godalming, he must have arranged that fixture.[3]

William Hayman occasionally acted as an umpire, but

there is no evidence from either England or Australia that he ever played in the team, despite his nonchalant bat-under-arm pose in the celebrated Warrnambool group photograph (Plate 24). His normal role was team scorer. In later years, Hayman's son presented the tour's 'Lillywhite's Registered Score Book' to the Hamilton Mechanics' Institute and this valuable record is preserved in the Glenelg Regional Library, Hamilton. Unfortunately, the other records in the possession of the Hayman family were destroyed in a fire many years ago. Hayman's loyalty to his team is revealed in his scrawled comment across the Sussex match record: 'Drawn match in consequence of the rain. The Brighton men refused to play. Afraid of being beaten!!!'

The Aborigines won 14 matches and lost the same number. It is apparent from the score book, however, that several of the 19 drawn games resulted from the weather's intervention on their behalf. Apparently the team only batted first on 11 occasions. This is surprising, as many clubs still followed the convention of allowing the visiting team first use of the wicket. Tossing the coin to decide the issue was an innovation (Tom Wills introduced it to Victoria in 1858), but even with a toss of the coin the Aborigines should have fared better. Perhaps Lawrence was diplomatic. He did call correctly when the coin was tossed at Bramhall Lane, but despite favourable conditions he sent the Sheffield team to the wicket to bat first (Plate 25).

The Aborigines practised hard in their new surroundings before their first English engagement, against Surrey at the Oval on 25 and 26 May. Evidently, they adjusted well and they were accepted by the West Malling community. Lawrence recalled an incident when the Aborigines paid a visit to the draper's shop.[4] Lawrence arrived later at the shop, where the proprietor invited him 'into the drawing room as his daughters were amusing my gentlemen with a little music. I thanked him and went in. Three of the Blacks were reclining upon sofas whilst the ladies were playing and sing-

1.The first All-England XI to visit Australia, 1861–62. Charles Lawrence is sitting at bottom right and William Caffyn stands in centre row, ball in hand.

2. The arrival of the first All-England XI at the Café de Paris, Bourke Street, Melbourne, December 1861. The owners, Spiers and Pond, sponsored the tour at a cost of £7000, and their profit enabled them to return to London and establish a flourishing West End restaurant.

3. The Melbourne Cricket Ground photographed in 1860 during an intercolonial match between Victoria and New South Wales. A hot north wind was blowing and the hard, parched ground appears virtually ungrassed. The Governor, Sir Henry Barkly, was a spectator in his box in the centre of the canvas covered stand. This was a posed photograph: the players stood in a state of suspended animation for some time.

4. Cricket: the bush ideal. 'Boy Playing Cricket', a painting by John Michael Crossland, 1854. Nannultera was a pupil at the Missionary Institute of Poonindie, South Australia. It possibly pictures the first evidence for Aboriginal cricketers.

5. The first international match at the MCG, New Year's Day 1862, when the All-England XI played a Victorian XVIII. The refreshment tents catered for a crowd of 15,000 spectators. The Spiers and Pond name is visible centre right. To the left is the tent of Rowley, presumably the sponsor of the first Aboriginal match in December 1866.

6.
Cricket: bush reality. Aboriginal cricketers at an unknown location.

A. Map of western Victoria.

7. The Deebing Creek Aboriginal station team was successful in the south-eastern Queensland cricket competition during the 1890s. The team was photographed for *The Queenslander*, 16 June 1894.

9.
Cricket match at Coranderrk
Aboriginal station, Healesville,
Victoria, about 1877. From an
album of views taken by 'Fred
Kruger (Gold Medallist) of
Geelong', dated 1878–80. The
English naturalist H.N. Moseley
visited Coranderrk a few years
previously and noted a craze for
cricket among the Aborigines.

8.

Aborigines at cricket, Point Macleay, South Australia. The photograph probably was taken by George Taplin, missionary at Point Macleay from 1859 to 1879. A date in the early 1870s is probable. The bowler is apparently about to bowl a round-arm (below shoulder) delivery.

10. 'The Invincibles', formed by H.S. Lefroy at New Norcia in the late 1870s and successful in Perth cricket for the following quarter of a century. This was the original team, photographed in about 1879. The 'pillbox' cap was popular even with contemporary English cricketers. The names of the team members are as follows, but their identification is less certain. Alternative spelling in brackets. Standing at rear, left to right — Patrick Yapo, John Walley, Benedict Caper (Kuper), Anthony Nelabut, Alec Wegnola (Wanola), captain; sitting left centre, James Egan; sitting front row, left to right, Paul Jater (Jiatter), John Blurton, H. S. Lefroy, Frederick Yrbel, Joseph Nogolot; sitting lower front right, Felix Jackimara.

11. Prehistoric Aboriginal eel fishery at Toolondo, near Mount Talbot. This artificial channel connected two swamps across a rise, maintaining their water level. Eel traps were placed along the 3.75 kilometres of this channel.

12. Cricket dress, 1890. The cricketing tradition continued at Coranderrk. This studio portrait of the prominent player, Sampson Barber, provides a clear view of contemporary bat and pads. (Merle Jacomos).

13. Mount Talbot homestead, erected during the early 1860s, when Aboriginal station hands were learning cricket under C. M. Officer's direction. The building is on the Register of the National Estate.

14. A cricket match in progress during the 1890s in a paddock near Mount Talbot homestead. This is presumably where the Aborigines played.

ARRIVAL OF THE BLACK CRICKETERS.

Since the late ingenious George Martin brought Deerfoot from America to contend against English pedestrians no arrival has been anticipated with so much curiosity and interest as that of the Black Cricketers from Australia. It has been already stated that the team had sailed from Sydney in the Paramatta, and that they were expected to reach our shores in May. We have now to record the fact that they landed at Gravesend last Wednesday, and on the following day exhibited their cricket prowess at Town Malling, in Kent, in the presence, among others, of Mr. W. S. Norton, the honorary secretary of the Kent County Club, and we hear that they gave great satisfaction to a critical *coterie* of spectators. They are thirteen in number, and are captained by Charles Lawrence, late of the All-England Eleven, who has been for some time at the antipodes. We append their native names, and opposite is given their *soubriquets*, under which they will doubtless be known here:—

Jungunjinanuke	Dick-a-Dick
Arrahmunijarrimun	Peter
Unaarrimin	Mullagh
Zellanach	Cuzens
Ballrinjarrimin	Sundown
Brippokei	King Cole
Bonnibarngeet	Tiger
Brimbunyah	Red Cap
Bullchanach	Bullocky
Grougarrong	Mosquito
Jallachmurrimin	Jim Crow
Murrumgunarriman	Twopenny
Pripumuarraman	Charley Dumas

They are the first Australian natives who have visited this country on such a novel expedition, but it must not be inferred that they are savages; on the contrary, the managers of the speculation make no pretence to anything other than purity of race and origin. They are perfectly civilised, having been brought up in the bush to agricultural pursuits as assistants to Europeans, and the only language of which they have a perfect knowledge is English. Monday in the Derby week (May 25) is to witness their *début* in London, arrangements having been made for them to play their first match against Eleven Gentlemen of the Surrey Club, at the Oval, on May 25 and 26; and on the Thursday after the Derby they will go through a series of athletic exorcises on the Surrey ground. The following gentlemen of the Surrey Club have been selected to play against the Blacks in their first match:—

I. D. Walker	W. L. Holt	C. Noble
R. Baggallay	R. Boultbee	W. Hibberd
G. M. Kelson	R. Burton	— Waitson
R. Troughton	H. Jupp	

In addition, the Blacks are engaged to play Eleven Gentlemen of Kent, at Gravesend, on Whit Monday, Tuesday, and Wednesday, the following being the Kent names selected:—

W. S. Norton	C. B. Griffith	E. A. White
M. A. Troughton	W. Lindsay	F. Ray
G. M. Kelson	R. Lipscomb	Captain Boycott
P. Hilton	R. B. Cooper	

Matches have also been arranged to take place at Nottingham, Sheffield, Manchester, Bradford, Halifax, Dewsbury, Portsmouth, and Hastings. With respect to their prowess as cricketers—that will be conclusively determined by their first public match. We hear, however, that Cuzens and Mullagh show considerable talent and precision in bowling, but, to use a homely phrase—the proof of the pudding will be in the eating.

B. 'Arrival of the black cricketers' (from *Sporting Life* (London), 16 May 1868).

15. Log lock-up, erected in Harrow around 1859. It is constructed of rough-hewn logs stacked 14 high, with the logs crossed and half-notched at the corners; the ceiling also consists of logs. A fairly standard design then, this rare example is on the Register of the National Estate.

16. 'Minjah in the Oldtime', a painting from the mid-1860s by Robert Dowling. It portrays the romantic nostalgia for the rapidly declining Aboriginal population. The Aboriginal team travelled through Minjah in 1867 and stayed overnight at nearby Greenhills station.

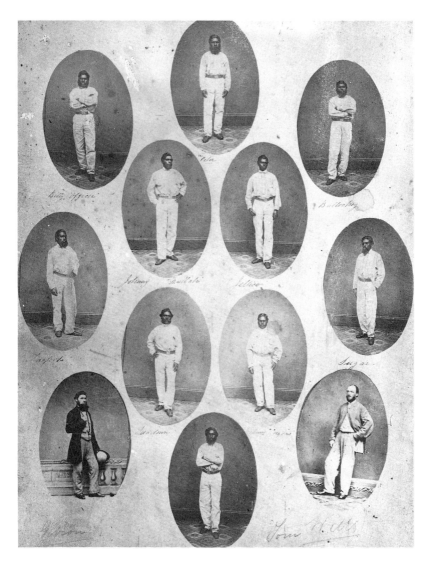

17. The earliest known photograph of the Aboriginal team, presumably dating from October–November 1866 and sent to Melbourne for forward publicity. The fact that the floor pattern is the same for all the Aborigines but different behind the two Europeans suggests that the latter photographs were added to the montage. The Aborigines probably were photographed by Kruger in Hamilton during their match there, weeks before Tom Wills arrived to coach them. Top row, left to right, Billy Officer, Peter, Bullocky; centre, Tarpot, Mullagh, Jellico, Sugar; lower centre, Sundown, Cuzens; bottom row, Gibson (umpire/backer), Neddy, Tom Wills.

18. The first Aboriginal cricket team. Although published in the *Australian News* (Melbourne) on 20 December 1866, close inspection shows that these figures are mirror images adapted by the etcher from the photograph in Plate 17. Consequently, the photo was several weeks old and Sugar had died, while Neddy did not play.

19.
The Aboriginal cricketers at the Melbourne Cricket Ground on Boxing Day, 1866. The pavilion at left features in later team photographs.

20. The Albert Ground, Redfern, opened in 1864, three years before the Aborigines played there. Charles Lawrence was a coach to the Albert Club, whose ground was then the best in Sydney. This view dates from 1874, when the All-England XI led by W. G. Grace was playing. The small pavilion, extreme left, was almost identical in design to the MCG pavilion.

21. The team captained by Wills, December 1866. This photograph was taken alongside the pavilion of the MCG, although records claim it to be a photograph at the Albert Club, Redfern. The team members: at rear (left to right), Tarpot, T. W. Wills, Mullagh; front row, King Cole (leg on chair), Dick-a-Dick (standing); seated (left to right), Jellico, Peter, Red Cap, Harry Rose, Bullocky, Cuzens.

22. The team with the same hats, photographed at the same place, but with different company. As this photograph was by Paterson Brothers of Bourke Street, Melbourne, the location was the Melbourne Cricket Ground. A record at Lord's identifies Wills as extreme left, Hayman extreme right and Captain W. E. Brougham Gurnett as the top-hatted centre man.

C. Sports at Trent Bridge Ground, 5 August 1868 (by courtesy of the Nottinghamshire County Cricket Club).

23. The team under Wills (top left) photographed at Ballarat in January 1867.

24. The Aboriginal team in England in 1868 with Lawrence holding a bat. This otherwise unlabelled photograph was reproduced by W. G. Grace in his autobiography *W. G.*

25. The second tour team photographed at Warrnambool in October 1867 by P. Dawson of Hamilton. The *Warrnambool Examiner* (8 October) described it as follows: 'the picture is 18 inches by 24 inches, the portraits being formed into an oval mounted on cardboard, the borders beautifully lithographed in black and gold...the style is in elegant taste and reflects great credit' upon the photographer. Top, G. Smith; second row, King Cole, Dick-a-Dick, Tiger, Mosquito; third row, H. Rose, Cuzens, Charles Lawrence, Red Cap; fourth row, Sundown, Twopenny, Jim Crow, Peter; central figures, Mullagh, Bullocky; bottom, W. Hayman.

26. The sailing ship *Parramatta* on which the team sailed to England in 1868.

27. The match in progress at Derby, September 1868. Possibly Twopenny is batting;
note the number of fieldsmen supporting the wicket-keeper. No wicket has been
prepared, although the grass is short across the field. The bowler-hatted
fieldsman, extreme left, is John Smith, whose bowling wrecked both Aboriginal
innings. Note the general rural appearance.

28. The Aboriginal team about to take the field at Trent Bridge, Nottingham, August 1868. From information supplied by Mr John Knott, Sydney, the team identification is as follows: standing (left to right), Dick-a-Dick, Tiger, Mullagh, Lawrence, Cuzens, Red Cap, Bullocky, Twopenny; seated, Mosquito, Peter, W. Shepherd, Dumas.

29. The colourfully attired Nottinghamshire Commercial team which drew with the Aborigines at Trent Bridge in August 1868. Standing (left to right), A. Fewkes, C. F. Daft, A. Poyser (umpire), T. Wright, G. M. Royle, G. Rossall, W. Clements, R. Tolley; seated, J. West, S. Brittle, W. T. Palmer, J. Billyeald.

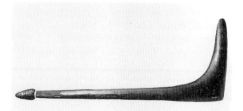

30. The leowell, or club, owned by Dick-a-Dick and used to ward off cricket balls. In his left hand he held a narrow parrying shield. These two carved wooden artefacts were the traditional weapons used in western Victoria, so Dick-a-Dick was adept in their use.

31.

Harry Rose, photographed at Mount Talbot with the station's prize imported merino ram. Beside him is the elaborate silver cup won by C. and S. Officer at the first Upper Glenelg and Wimmera Pastoral Society Show, held at Balmoral in August 1864.

32.

Johnny Cuzens, probably photographed in 1869 during the period of his employment by the Melbourne Cricket Club.

33.

Portrait of Mullagh in a European setting. Formerly hanging in the Harrow Mechanics' Institute, it was destroyed in a fire some years ago.

34.

Mullagh photographed in post-tour days, by which time he had become a district celebrity. This dignified man presumably wears the watch and chain which he had won in England.

35. William Hayman in later life.

36. Metal plaque (70 mm by 50 mm) found in 1950 at Kitticoola mine, in the Adelaide hills. It is testimony to the popularity of the Aboriginal team. Around the 1860s colourful belts were worn with attractive buckles (compare the belt worn by Cuzens in Plate 31). Many buckles depicted cricketing themes and one English motif proclaimed that 'the prince and peasant by cricket are united'.

37. Mullagh's grave in Harrow cemetery. Erected by public subscription, the headstone is inscribed 'world famous cricketer'. The funeral was attended by people from as far distant as Hamilton.

38. *Right* The memorial erected in 1891 to Mullagh at Harrow's Mullagh Oval. Testimony at the time to Victorian sentiment, today the neglected ground testifies to social changes in rural Victoria.

39. The 1951 memorial in the Edenhope High School grounds. Here, on the shore of Lake Wallace, the Aboriginal cricketers were coached by Tom Wills and Charles Lawrence.

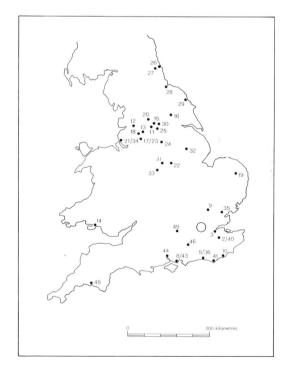

D. Team fixtures in England, 1868, in order of games played. Ten fixtures were staged in the London area. (1, 3, 4, 6, 7, 37–9, 42, 47).

Ba 78/74
Rec 6/6/76. Aboriginal Station
Framlingham
2nd June 1876

Mr Andrews

Dear Sir

I write to you
with the intention
of bringing under your
notice that I have
been working on the
Station this last six
years. and never received
any payment for the
same. doing Carpenter

work. and I wish to
let you know if they
intend giving me any
thing for my work
I would prefer a double
barreled gun for the
money I have made
a Bullock Dray wheel
for the Dray. Please
write as soon as
convenient

I remain your
true servant
James Cousins

E.
Letter from James Cousins
(Mosquito) written at the
Framlingham Aboriginal
settlement, 2 June 1876 (by
courtesy of the Victorian State
Archives).

ing. They all seemed delighted with the evening's amusement and promised to call again'.

The day of the match dawned fine and the team travelled by train to London. On their way through Kennington in time for a noon start to the game, they made a ceremonial media publicity halt at the factory of E. J. Page, where each player received 'a cane-handled bat and a copy of the *Cricketer's Pocket Book*'. Some 7000 spectators were at the Oval, 'among whom were several ladies...in carriages and on horseback'. Cuzens was ill with enteritis and unable to play. Despite his absence, the team impressed the critics from the popular press, who employed superlatives to describe the match. 'A new epoch in the history of cricket,' prophesied *Reynold's News*; 'decidedly the event of the century,' trumpeted the *Sheffield Telegraph*; 'not a third-rate batsman amongst them' was the final opinion of *Reynold's News*. *The Times* took a contrary view — 'second-rate bowling', batting was 'sadly wanting in power', while running between wickets was slow and hesitant.

Surrey won the toss and batted in sunshine, while Mullagh and Lawrence opened the bowling attack. When Mullagh bowled, Lawrence fielded at mid-off, and Charley Dumas at mid-on. King Cole was placed at point, Dick-a-Dick at cover point, Peter at third man and Jim Crow at short-leg. Behind the wicket, Bullocky doubled as wicket-keeper and first slip. To support him, Red Cap was placed deep in slips, Tiger at long leg, while Twopenny was 'long stop — very clever'.

Before play started, the Aborigines gave three cheers, ending with an ear-piercing whoop, which delighted the crowd. An interested spectator recalled that they played bare-footed 'and ran like deer. Their running between wickets could be heard as well as seen. They tore up and down the pitch, screaming and shouting native back-chat'. In the field, their enthusiasm reminded him of 'a lot of children', who 'gave good entertainment and the game was never slow'.

Lawrence, who took seven wickets, and Mullagh with

three victims accounted for the opposition but not before they scored 222 runs. Ten of the Surrey team were first-class cricketers and most of them contributed solid performances. King Cole and Bullocky also bowled, although without success. Bullocky stumped two players, before he handed the wicket-keeping task over to Mullagh. While fielding at mid-off, Bullocky ran to take the best catch of the match, thereby making up for Peter, who dropped an easy chance. The Aborigines all bowled over-arm, although Lawrence successfully changed to underarm slows for a time (Plates 25 & 26).

In their first innings, the Aborigines totalled only 83, of which Mullagh scored 33 and King Cole 14. Forced to follow on, the team made 132, 73 of the total being contributed by Mullagh. At a time before boundaries became a convention, Mullagh's three fours were all run. He was at the wickets for 80 minutes, 60 of them with Peter, who held out with 'quaint and dogged' defence for his four runs. Consequently, the Aborigines lost their first match by an innings and seven runs. Mullagh, however, was chaired and cheered off the ground and rewarded with a cash prize for his performance. It was a pleasing game for the spectators, who included the Marquis of Hastings, and all press critics were satisfied, except *The Times* representative. It also pleased the promoters and Surrey secretary, Burrup. During these two days and a very successful third day of sports, more than 20,000 people attended the Oval, and paid £603.2.6 admittance. Burrup received £150 on behalf of the club, the local police received £20 for keeping the peace and each umpire was one pound richer. After all expenses were paid, Graham's accounting entries indicate that the syndicate profited by £309.9.1. It was a promising tour opener.[5]

The team's appearance on 30 May for a one-day match against the aristocratic Mote Park Club enhanced its reputation. The Maidstone fixture was a village green public relations exercise set in a rural deer park, before 'a more numerous and more fashionable attendance than we ever remember'. While two military bands played, almost 80 people drawn from the local social register lunched with the team. Although the home team scored 151, the visitors were a promising four wickets for 119 when play ended to allow time for the Aboriginal sports. Cuzens had recovered and celebrated by scoring 21 and capturing two wickets. Despite its meagre profit of £16.5.0, the syndicate must have felt satisfied. The stamp of respectability was on the tour. The Marylebone Cricket Club must have noted that Lord Paget and other county gentry participated in the match, that the club president attended the lunch and that the standard of cricket was praised. The *Maidstone Journal* remarked upon this memorable occasion, with 'the great novelty of seeing men of colour play (a thing by many thought at one time impossible)'.[6] More than a century later, in 1973, this attractive setting witnessed M. C. Cowdrey score his hundredth first-class century.

The tour obviously created considerable interest and, due to the care taken by Lawrence and Hayman to cement good relations with the press and with Kent and Surrey cricket authorities, the Aborigines were welcomed. English press coverage was good at the start of the tour. However, comments became less frequent and were normally reserved for the matches played within the area of the paper's circulation. *The Times* published accounts of the first Oval match and the one at Lord's, whereupon it pronounced that Aboriginal play was 'a travestie upon cricket', and ignored the team thereafter. Unfortunately, some of the potentially most illuminating sources for following the fortunes of the tour proved disappointing. *Wisden*'s record merely listed all fixtures and results but offered no general comment or evaluation of players. The *Illustrated London News* and *Punch* both overlooked an event which could have provided rich copy. That invaluable compendium *Cricket Scores and Biographies* only reproduced the scores for almost all matches, with an occasional factual addendum. *John Lillywhite's Cricketers' Companion* made only a single mention of the tour.

The team was well received, a conclusion supported alike

by generally favourable newspaper reportage and by the fact that although only 10 matches were arranged initially, and the team was scheduled to return in August, they remained until October. Newspapers were patronizing at times, but not to the extent of some Australian papers, and normally they reported matches in similar vein to ordinary fixtures. Half a column or more was devoted to a day's account.

Lawrence may have used his All-England XI prestige and contacts to good purpose at the start of the tour in cultivating the theme that his men were upright Victorian sportsmen. There is a remarkable similarity in detail and phraseology between several papers, suggestive of a prepared publicity hand-out. For example, two opposing poles of journalism, *The Times* and *Sporting Life*, used identical phrases to describe these 'perfectly civilized', English-speaking, agricultural workers. Far from London, the *Yorkshire Post* repeated these concepts (Figure C). It may have been calculated publicity which led Lawrence to launch the team at the Oval during Derby week, and he took them to the Derby, where they shared the limelight with royalty. The social contacts of the team early in its English visit must have overcome many ethnic barriers.[7] Later that century, Andrew Lang, the celebrated popular writer on folklore and ethnology, expressed an opinion of Australian Aborigines which may epitomise the attitude of many people in 1868. 'They were adroit hunters, skilled trackers, born sportsmen,' he concluded, 'they now ride well, and, for savages, play cricket fairly.'[8] It is likely that, in many English clubs of the day, the same comment was made of white Australians, only 'colonials' would have been substituted for 'savages'.

The men of the press certainly were cultivated by the sponsors. Hayman and Hingston extended invitations to visit West Malling to watch the team practice. Charles Box, who may have seen them there, noted their 'manly and dignified bearing'. The *Field* correspondent, W. B. Tegetmeier, watched the Aborigines practice and went on to dine and to play cribbage with them. All these activities were duly described for the public and good press relations were maintained throughout the tour. At the end of September, W. S. Norton and a team of press critics took the field for a challenge match on the Earl of Romney's Mote Park ground, Maidstone. Rain prevented a result, but the publicity was useful, for one paper congratulated the tour promoters 'on the success of their interesting experiment'. The burden of all the early press commentary emphasized the good standard of cricket played by these 'civilized' Aborigines, all of whom spoke English.

With men of the influence of W. Burrup and W. S. Norton supporting the tourists, together with the partly orchestrated press publicity, the sponsors achieved a high profile. They also derived notice from the patronage of a former Governor of New South Wales, Sir William Denison, who attended the match at Richmond Deer Park. He presented each Aboriginal with 10 shillings, continuing an interest in Australian cricket which began when he granted permission for games to be played in Sydney's Domain. They also won over the reluctant Marylebone Cricket Club. The MCC committee initially refused to allow a match at Lord's, but this decision was reversed after the team's arrival. Even then, any display of native or athletic sports was forbidden, but staging that match conveyed status on the tour (Figure B). The final accolade was bestowed some years later by the editor of *Cricket Scores and Biographies*. He considered that the inclusion of Aboriginal tour results among English official fixtures of the 1868 season needed justification, in light of the exclusion of later professional cricket results. 'It may here be stated,' the editor explained, 'though the Blacks' matches are all here inserted, the matches played by the Clown Elevens, subsequently started, have no place in these pages. The former was an interesting performance, but the latter a mere farce.'[9]

This verdict was qualified, however, because the editor

added that the team was only 'occasionally pitted against some very good Gentlemen Elevens'. How good was the opposition faced by the tourists? A partial answer is available in the results provided in *Scores and Biographies*, Volume X, 1867–68. Seven teams were played which correspond with familiar county teams today, although not in standard. These teams were Hampshire, Kent, Marylebone Cricket Club, Middlesex, Surrey, Sussex and Yorkshire. At the other extreme, 20 of those teams which challenged the Aborigines were not again reported in *Scores and Biographies*. It must be assumed that they were assessed as poor in both status and standard. The remaining 14 teams were published in other contexts. Although an oddly assorted group, they may be ranged notionally somewhere between the county teams and the rest. These clubs were the following: Bishop Stortford, Bootle, Bradford, East Hampshire, Godalming, Hastings, Lincoln, Nottingham Commercial, The Press, Reading, Richmond, Scarborough and Sheffield. As the Swansea club fielded what was effectively a representative South Wales team, probably it should be added to this group.

Using this combination of thumb as rule and fingers as calculator, the following graded results were obtained. They suggest that the Aboriginal team fits around the middle grade in this arbitrary hierarchy.

	Teams	Matches	Won	Drawn	Lost
County	7	10	—	4	6
Mid-grade	14	16	5	8	3
Minor	20	21	9	6	5
Total	41	47	14	18	14

A further variant is to examine individual feats of prowess. Three centuries were scored against the Aborigines (121, 117, 100) and the best performance with the ball was the six wickets for 28 runs taken by A. J. Smith in the first innings for South Derbyshire (four wickets with consecutive balls), followed by his six wickets for 16 runs (including another hat-trick) in the second innings (Plate 28). These were better performances than individual Aboriginal efforts, although only Smith's bowling was overwhelmingly superior. Two contemporary English cricketers offered general assessments of their standard. W. G. Grace observed, somewhat patronizingly, that 'in strength they were about equal to third-class English teams; and the result of their visit was satisfactory and encouraging to them in every respect'. He praised Mullagh and Cuzens for their 'very good all-round form'. South Norton also praised these two as 'quite up to County form', but described the rest as 'very poor players, being boomerangers and spear throwers rather than cricketers'.[10]

In adopting an approach which assumes that the best English cricketers participated in such representative teams as North of England, the South, United All-England, or the team which toured America around that time, a list of the 33 most prominent players can be compiled. Of these only four took the field against the Aborigines — C. F. Buller, J. Grundy, R. Lipscomb and G. H. Jupp. There were several Jupps playing first-class cricket in England at the time and because their full initials are not always given in the scorebooks or match results, it is not possible to distinguish them. It is assumed that it was G. H. Jupp in each case.

C. F. Buller, an all-rounder, played for the MCC against the Aborigines at Lord's. In two innings he averaged 18.5 runs and captured eight wickets (average not known) with his slow round-arm bowling. At the time he was aged 23 years and was in his fourth season in Middlesex, so was in the prime of his career. In all, he played 24 first-class matches over 13 seasons with a batting average of 21.8 and a bowling average of 31.4. On balance his batting against the Aborigines' bowling was below his performance against other first-class bowling in England, but his bowling performance was far better.

G. H. Jupp played in five matches against the Aborigines and in six innings scored 89 runs (average 15). He would then have been 27 years of age and had been playing first-class cricket for seven seasons. He went on to play 252 first-class games, played Test cricket for England with a career average of 27 — much better than against the Aborigines while in his prime. F. Lipscomb was then 34 years of age and was a right-hand batsman and a slow bowler. In scoring only one run and taking four wickets he reflected the performance of Buller — not doing well with the bat but being well above the standard of his first-class performances with his slow bowling. J. Grundy was aged 44 in 1868, but was still an active first-class cricketer. His five runs in two innings against the Aborigines was well below his career average of just under 13.

This analysis suggests that the Aboriginal bowling was up to first-class standard but their batting was more susceptible to slow bowling than other English cricketers in first-class matches. No doubt the latter was made more dramatic with the complete failure of the last three or four Aboriginal batsmen. The top order were certainly of first-class calibre. Lawrence was already in the upper bracket of first-class cricketers, and Mullagh, Cuzens, Bullocky and Twopenny played fleetingly at that standard in Australian intercolonial competition.

The English Association of Cricket Statisticians recently compiled a list of all first-class matches played in England from which a 'Who's Who' of first-class cricketers in England has been published. None of the Aboriginal team's matches is included in the first-class listing, thus no Aboriginal appears in the list of first-class cricketers playing in the British Isles. The 10 matches against the seven 'county' teams must have come close to first-class standard and it is to be regretted that Mullagh, Cuzens and Twopenny, at least, will never be known as first-class cricketers in England.

It must be remarked that the Australian XI which toured

England in 1879–80 played many of the same clubs and,
upon their arrival, no arrangements had been made for
fixtures at Lord's or the Oval. Their agent advertised in the
press that they were willing to play 'any team that they liked
to bring against us'. These included XVIIIs from clubs familiar to the Aborigines, including Longsight, Rochdale,
Keighley, Middlesborough, Scarborough and Hastings. The
Aborigines should not be dismissed as being of inferior
standard for playing a similar circuit.[11]

Sports writers attempted to describe the physical appearance of the Aborigines with an objectivity superior to that of
many contemporary anthropologists. In this touring year,
1868, the great evolutionary champion T. H. Huxley pro-
pounded his influential systematization of the 'Races of Man-
kind'. In the course of this classification he made a superficial and dubious comparison between Aborigines and
southern Indian sailors 'such as may be seen among the crew
of any recently returned East Indiaman'. The fieldwork of
sporting critics on the playing fields of Rochdale, Newcastle,
Sheffield and London was superior to this generalization.
They offered descriptions of Aboriginal physique and stature
and commented upon their gentle and 'by no means unintel-
lectual' appearance, their 'long and wiry beards', and 'manly, dignified, and pleasantly confident gait and bearing'. The
Newcastle Daily Chronicle observed that Aboriginal stature
'differed as much as the same number of Englishmen taken
at random' might vary, and was 'particularly struck by the
smart, lively and gentlemanly appearance of the men'. As
described earlier, the *Field* reproduced a series of physical
measurements of Cuzens, Charley Dumas and Dick-a-Dick
as a matter of objective record. The same feature quoted
Herbert Spencer's 'survival of the fittest' with regret, in
supporting its conclusion that an Aboriginal team would
never return to England, because the race was destined for
extinction, like the Tasmanian race, which was then in public notice.

Another piece stressed errors in popular belief, which assumed Aboriginal society was 'scarcely above the level of brute creation'. It found that the team's 'general behaviour, either at meals or in conversation, is quite equal to many beings who consider themselves highly civilised'. As the *Rochdale Observer* expressed it, they were 'stalwart men'.

North Country interest and sympathy may have been partly satisfied reaction to the success of a black race. A few years earlier the common people felt the economic effects of the American Civil War which drastically curtailed the cotton industry. Despite great distress, there was strong humanitarian and radical support for the Negro slaves upon whose labour the cotton crop depended. The arrival of the Aborigines in the cotton towns must have sparked some enthusiasm for a racial underdog. (When they played in Rochdale it was the brass band from Healey Hall cotton mill which supplied the background noises.)

There were other important intellectual influences. A Sheffield writer made a significant racial diagnosis when he remarked that 'contrary to general expectation, the Aboriginal team turned out to be a fine body of men'. He considered them to be 'not only far removed from the low, negro type of *genus homo*, but able to "take their own part" with well developed Europeans'.

Perhaps this was the secret of their success: they played cricket, and they looked so much like Europeans at a distance that they needed coloured sashes to distinguish them. It might be concluded that the tourists were seen as virtual photographic negatives of white cricketers.[12] It is interesting that Daisy Bates was later to employ a similarly racial and racist interpretation to explain why Western Australian Aboriginal cricketers were accepted by the white community. 'This understanding camaraderie in clean British sport,' she believed, 'oddly supports the now generally accepted belief that the Australian Aborigines were black Caucasians, and thus distant "cousins" of our own.' An earlier report on the Wills team's appearance at Bathurst on Boxing Day, 1867, reflected the same British ethnocentricity:

> Truly, we cannot help thinking that cricket has a humanising and civilizing influence, for Mr Lawrence's black team observe all the courtesies and amenities of the cricketing field and privately both act and speak like gentlemen.

The editor of the *Ballarat Star* rationalized the social position of the Aborigines when Wills captained the first team during its visit to Ballarat:[13]

> The order of civilisation in the Christian sense seems to be first to make savages men and then to make them Christians...To convert the savage into a sheep shearer was something, but it is more to make him into a smart cricketer...the savage rises to quite a higher social level. He is at once brought out into a wider arena of action and thought, but into contact with...wholesome influences generally...with its requirements of agility, nerve, self-possession, obedience to law, and [when we] see him in contact with a superior race, in physical rivalry with his civilisers under the healthiest conditions practicable, we must conclude that something has been done to elevate him above his natural level as a savage.

As previously mentioned, the Marylebone Cricket Club committee voted against staging a match at Lord's but reversed its decision after the opening of the tour. They persisted in their ruling against any sports exhibition, but despite their wishes the Aborigines provided the enthusiastic crowd with a demonstration in the use of weapons. In discussion after the event the committee decided that no great harm had been done. However, its agreement had been purchased at a price. It must be inferred from Graham's statement of accounts for this match that the MCC received half the gross receipts. This was 25 per cent above the concession at the Oval, or any other ground, although they evidently paid the accommodation and incidental expenses of the visitors.

Despite the meagre profit margin, this historic match was an extraordinary example of amicable racial relations. The MCC team included an earl, a viscount, a lieutenant-colonel and a captain. The Earl of Coventry had been the MCC president in 1859, and Viscount Downe was destined for the same office in 1872. Lieutenant-Colonel Bathurst had represented Eton and played for Hampshire.[14] Probably no group of Aboriginal people ever mixed with the top of the social register in European Australia until the past decade (see Figure B).

Information provided in the 1869 edition of *Wisden* permits an illuminating analysis of Marylebone Cricket Club fixtures during the 1868 season. As *Wisden* designated this match 'MCC' versus 'The Australians', this fact merits record. MCC played 16 other matches at Lord's and eight fixtures elsewhere. In terms of the social register, the Aborigines were among prestigious company. The other Lord's matches included eight county and three university and public school teams, the Royal Artillery, Gentlemen of Ireland, England, Colts of England and Civil Service. Aboriginal status in the social register was enhanced by the prestige of their opponents. The earl did not play in any other fixture, the viscount played only in two other matches, while the lieutenant-colonel outranked all other nine officers who took the field that season.

The match analysis for all other fixtures described the team as 'MCC and Ground', presumably indicating that on all other occasions Lord's ground staff participated. These professionals carried out the burden of the bowling, taking more than 80 per cent of all wickets. It may be concluded that by not playing ground staff against the Aborigines, MCC felt there was no possibility of losing the match. On the other hand, the social standing of the substitutes suggests a compliment to 'The Australians'; certainly they were not snubbed.[15]

Despite the disapproval of *The Times*, the team's performance was creditable until their disastrous second innings, linked with the intriguing absence of Bullocky. MCC scored 164 and 120. Cuzens's total of wickets for the match was 10, from 60 overs, at a cost of 117 runs; Mullagh's bowling analysis was 8 wickets for 101 runs from 62 overs. Bathurst twice fell without scoring, a victim to Cuzens's bowling. In their first innings the Aborigines scored 185. Mullagh top scored with 75 and 'sundries' came next with 31; Bullocky, present at this stage, contributed 11 runs. When they returned to the crease, however, they collapsed for 45, of which Cuzens made 21 and Mullagh 12. An allusion to the recently revised rule which permitted overarm delivery is contained in a newspaper comment. Cuzens's fast bowling, 'whose delivery is of the windmill description and consequently somewhat dangerous on the Lord's wicket, proved very effective'. The fact that of the 39 wickets which fell, 29 were bowled probably indicates the poor wicket conditions, with erratic and low 'shooters'.

Although W. G. Grace, the arch-Tory of the cricket field, did not compete against the Aborigines, he watched them play. If he had thought them to be charlatans he would have said so. Instead he acknowledged that they had 'acquitted themselves very well' and that some had shown 'conspicuous skill at the game'. He went so far as to include in his memoirs a blurred photograph of the team standing before a tent (Plate 25). From fleeting evidence such as this it seems fair to conclude that the Aborigines were received on terms as equal as any accorded colonials in Victorian England, and rather better than in their homeland. From the praise heaped upon Cuzens for his innings of 43 at Trent Bridge, for example, it is evident that the *Nottingham Guardian* reflected popular opinion. There is a sense of authenticity in the statement that Cuzens received 'a thorough and genuine ovation' for his efforts.[16]

The disparity between the cricketing standards of a few of the players and the rest is patently obvious in the tour averages (Appendix II). Some were makeweight replacements, while others such as Charley Dumas paid their way with demonstrations of their extra-cricketing prowess with weapons. However, the number of occasions upon which even the weakest members took the field is an indication of their dedication and physical fitness or of the iron will of their managers. To judge from the scorebook, Bullocky's absence at Lord's was an exceptional occurrence.

The *Yorkshire Gazette* judged the team to be substandard. 'Their fielding and bowling is indifferent, their batting is devoid of science, and they seldom succeed in stopping the ball.' *The Times* proved equally critical. While such observations were partly justified they overlooked comparable weaknesses in the opposing sides. The Aborigines were seldom overwhelmed by their opposition, and at Reading it was the home side which sent down 20 wides, and lost by an innings and 218 runs. When Twopenny hit his record-making 'niner', the fielding team deserved most credit for the stroke. It was at Bramhall Lane (Sheffield) that Twopenny drove the ball past mid-on, 'and Mr Foster who was well up, did not offer for some time to go for the ball, and when started it was at a slow pace, the result being that nine was run for the hit amidst vociferous cheering'. It is relevant that a press critic judged Bullocky to be 'good enough to play in any of our county elevens'.

Other commentators found much to praise. It is interesting to note that 'Longstop', no admirer of the team, wrote after their return to Melbourne that he 'was astonished at the great progress the Blacks have made... They seem to have picked up the science of the game'. The Surrey Club presented its first 'talent' sovereign of the season to Mullagh for his scores of 33 and 73, while its last award of that season went to Cuzens, for his 63 runs and four wickets in their third match at the Oval. In this first match at the Oval Mullagh remained at the crease for 130 minutes in compiling his 73 runs. The players picked up other bonuses, as when Mullagh received a cup for his 94 at Reading, 50 shillings at Bootle, and eight guineas and a fob watch at Brighton. Such awards were not always merited. At Lewisham, Red Cap top-scored with 12 in an innings of only 42, and won a cup.[17]

In the team's outcricket, Mullagh, Cuzens and Lawrence dominated the game. Between them they bowled 4234 overs of the team's 4983 four-ball overs. Their tally of wickets was 609, while all other bowlers bagged only 105. With the aid of Bullocky these three also shared the task of wicket-keeping. Twopenny was credited on several occasions with being an excellent longstop, a position much in demand with rough pitches and erratic bowlers. Agile Dick-a-Dick brought off occasional brilliant catches, as with his 'splendid' one handed leaping dismissal at Sheffield, but generally there were many lapses of anticipation in the field and running after the ball was indifferent.

Field placings were orthodox and lacked the sophisticated experimentation which has characterized modern cricket. A standard field consisted of point, cover-point, third man, mid-off, mid-on, short-leg, long-leg, long-slip and longstop. Provided that the stroke was made, these placings should have ensured many easy singles. The only unusual field placement noted was that for Mullagh, when he bowled fast deliveries at Bury.[18] Except for a man at long-leg, all fieldsmen were on the off side, but 'from the few hits made on the on side the judiciousness of this arrangement was apparent'.

Full details of two innings, in which Mullagh apparently secured 12 wickets and Lawrence 7, have not been included in published team averages. These were the first innings at Rochdale and the second at North Shields. If these totals are included, both Mullagh and Lawrence took more than 250 wickets each at averages which seem beyond belief today — 10 and 12.1 respectively: 831 of Mullagh's 1877 overs were maidens. Cuzens secured 114 wickets at an average of 11.3. He was the fastest bowler and had the highest delivery. Mullagh took five wickets or more on no less than 24 occasions. He was the most consistent bowler for length and he varied his pace.

Twopenny was the surprise bowling find of the tour. He sent down only 176 overs and almost all of them late in the season. The 43rd and 44th matches were his triumphs. Against East Hampshire he had secured 9 wickets for 9 runs by his 11th over, and he caught the 10th victim. He then scored 11 runs, followed by another 5 wickets for 7 runs in the second innings. Hayman felt constrained to write across the score sheet: 'Twopenny's bowling was very good.' To confirm Hayman's faith in his abilities, Twopenny proceeded to Southampton and clean bowled nine opponents for 17 runs, in 21 overs. He failed to score but took three more wickets in the second innings. Curiously, although he played in the last three matches of the tour, Twopenny was asked to bowl only in the final one. Possibly he was injured, or perhaps rumours of 'chucking' led to an incident. After he returned to Australia some critics claimed that he threw the ball. His 35 wickets were taken at an average cost of 6.9 runs. The only other bowler with respectable figures was Red Cap whose 54 wickets cost 10.7 runs apiece. The bowling analysis of this tour is unlikely to be bettered, and on the entire round only three centuries were scored from their bowling.

The trio Lawrence, Mullagh and Cuzens also constituted the team's batting strength. All three scored more than 1000 runs on the tour, while Mullagh reached 1698 runs, at the best team average of 23.65. No centuries were scored by the tourists, although Mullagh hit 94 and Cuzens 87. Cuzens scored more than 50 on nine occasions and Mullagh on eight, while Lawrence reached his half-century in four innings. Mullagh was a steady player, who attempted to keep the ball down; Cuzens was more aggressive and took risks. Both batsmen were natural players and were as good as any of their opposition. The disparity in performance within the team is apparent here also. These three batsmen averaged 20 or better, while no other batsman averaged 10. Charley Dumas batted on 66 occasions, but amassed only 218 runs. Mosquito had a unique tour, being not out on 26 of his 46 visits to the crease; even so, his total was a meagre 77 runs. Peter failed to score on 17 out of 59 appearances at the wicket. Sundown travelled the equivalent of around the world to play in two matches and score a single run. Sundown's record was even more bizarre, because on the first Sydney tour under Tom Wills, he batted five times without ever scoring. He had a better average in Australian matches captained by Lawrence, when his seven games produced seven runs.

One of the curious features of the team was its batting order. There were numerous combinations of opening batsmen, and only once was the batting order of the first innings followed in the second. Bullocky, who had a reputation for stolid play, possibly came closest to the modern concept of the opener's role. To belie such confidence in his capabilities, however, is the fact that he was run out 13 times in 60 innings. Even Mullagh was liable to make ill-judged runs and impetuosity was a characteristic of the team. Of the 17 Aboriginal wickets to fall at Hove, five were run out. Frequent press comment also establishes that the Aborigines fared best when facing fast bowling and fell most commonly to the slow under-arm attack.

The journalist describing the Sussex match at Hove clearly enjoyed himself, but his own sense of rather patronizing fun also manages to highlight the individuality of the players and the manner in which they were involved in the game. His comments serve to indicate team weaknesses, at the same time providing insight into personalities.[19]

'Several of the eleven were rather sluggish in running between the wickets at which we were somewhat surprised, seeing their activity in other respects. Bullocky is really a very good bat. He was once nearly run out, and he created some mirth by his manifestations of pleasure at his narrow escape.' Bullocky was run out, however, in his second innings, when Mullagh stroked the ball at the other end and scattered the stumps at Bullocky's end. Bullocky was out of his crease and was given out, 'to his no small chagrin'. Dick-a-Dick proved 'an amusing fellow' and a hard hitter in making eleven runs; Twopenny proved 'another funny fellow' while partnering Lawrence, whose rapid run rate made Twopenny 'puff and blow in running'. When Lawrence was caught, 'young King Cole then went in, and scored 3 off the first ball. He and Twopenny were in for a considerable time, but the merry young soul was ultimately bowled' for 10 runs. Twopenny carried his bat for 10, but not before he partnered Charley Dumas and ran him out, for which Charley 'certainly did give...pepper for it, and no mistake'.

At the start of the tour, Cuzens was referred to as the team's best player. Although he continued to win praise, Mullagh soon supplanted him as the 'great' man of the team. Some of Mullagh's performances indicate a man possessing both skill and stamina. During the first innings at Hastings he captured three wickets for 47 runs, from 47.3 overs; 27 of these were maiden overs, 10 of which were bowled in succession. His second innings tally was two wickets for 88 runs, from 37 overs, including 21 maidens. When he batted, his two innings produced 23 and 72 runs. In the Sheffield match Mullagh was at the crease for two hours, while compiling 55 runs; he also delivered 49 overs, taking 5 wickets for 95 runs. His all-round versatility was climaxed in the victory at Burton-on-Trent in September. He top-scored in the first innings with 42, and in the match bowled four opponents in 38 overs for 59 runs and caught a fifth. He then donned the wicket-keeper's gloves and stumped four batsmen and caught one.

More than 30 years after the tour, Charles Lawrence recalled that the leading English fast bowler, George Tarrant, offered to give Mullagh batting practice during the luncheon break at one match. Not only was Mullagh so involved in batting against Tarrant that he missed his lunch, but Tarrant told Lawrence that Mullagh was 'one of the finest batsmen he had ever bowled against. . .'.

Latter-day all-rounders of the calibre of Gary Sobers or Keith Miller were no more versatile or energetic than was Mullagh, who carried a heavier load on tour than any modern team member. He bowled more than 37 per cent of all overs delivered and scored 22.25 per cent of his team's runs. He merited first-class status.[20]

Mullagh's obituary epitomizes the cricket of the team's star player: 'a fine, free wristy style and scientific defence, his hitting all round the wicket being hard and clean. As a bowler he would also have excelled had he not too closely imitated one of the first of his teachers, the celebrated T. W. Wills, and developed a tendency to shy. As a batsman against fast bowling, he had few. . .superiors, but like many of his sable compeers, he had a wholesome horror of "delusive slows".'

NOTES

[1] King Cole's death was referred to in several newspapers in such standardised terms that they must have used a news release, e.g. *Reynold's News*, 28 June 1868; C. Box, *The English Game of Cricket* (London, 1877), 324, attributed the death to pneumonia. Sundown and Jim Crow: *Aust.*, 26 December 1868, and *Cricket Scores and Biographies*, vol. 10, 363. The sympathetic correspondent: *Sporting Life*, 28 October 1868.

[2] The Hayman connection: personal communication from Sir Peter Hayman, Checkendon, Berkshire, England, 5 May 1968; Graham, Ledger, 6, 19, 127, 130 — unlabelled newspaper clippings provide details on W. S. Norton. Norton's comments, in Lord Harris (ed), *The History of Kent County Cricket* (London, 1907), 64.

[3] The Surrey Connection: Lawrence MS 1, pp 49, 66; Lord Alverstone and C. W. Alcock, *Surrey Cricket: Its History and Associations* (London, 1904), 322. Julius Caesar quotation, as described by R. Daft, *Kings of Cricket* (Bristol, [1893]), 56, 196. The fragmentary Surrey Cricket Club records are in the Surrey Record Office, Kingston-on-Thames, ref. 2042/8/8.

[4] Aborigines and draper's daughters: Lawrence MS 3.

[5] The Oval match is reconstructed from *Reynold's News*, 24 and 31 May 1868, *Sheffield Telegraph*, 26 May 1868, *The Times*, 26 May 1868. The field placings, *Sheffield Telegraph*. The interested spectator was Frank Gerald, *A Millionaire in Memories* (London, 1936), 212. Financial aspects: Graham, Ledger, 1–2.

[6] The Maidstone match is described in *Maidstone Journal*, 1 June 1868; Graham, Ledger, 3.

[7] *Cricket Scores and Biographies*, vol 10, includes the scores for almost all matches between pp 363 and 668. The team's initial reception by the press: *The Times*, 26 May 1868; *Sporting Life*, 16 May 1868; *Yorkshire Post*, 27 May 1868. *John Lillywhite's Cricketers' Companion for 1869* (London, 1869), 37.

[8] Andrew Lang's patronizing observation occurs in his introduction to K. Langloh Parker, *Australian Legendary Tales* (Melbourne, 1896).

[9] Relations with the press: C. Box, *The English Game of Cricket*, (London, 1877), 324; Graham, Accounts. The reaction of the MCC was explained in letter to Mulvaney by Miss D. Rait Kerr, Curator, MCC, 15 November 1966. The *Cricket Scores and Biographies'* explanation, vol 10, 363. The item about Sir William Denison came from the Lawrence papers.

[10] Playing standard: W. G. Grace, *Cricket* (London, 1891), 123; W. S. Norton, in Lord Harris (ed), *The History of Kent County Cricket* (London, 1907), 64.

[11] For the 1879–80 team fixtures, *Boyle and Scott's Australian Cricketers' Guide for 1879–80* (Melbourne, 1880), 167.

[12] Newspaper accounts referred to for their 'anthropology' include: *Rochdale Observer*, 4 July 1868; *Newcastle Daily Chronicle*, 19 August 1868; *Sheffield Telegraph*, 26 August 1868; *The Times*, 26 May 1868;

Graham, Accounts, 335. C. Box, *The English Game of Cricket* (London, 1877), 324.

13 Daisy Bates on cricket: *Aust.*, 12 January 1924, 94. Bathurst: *Aust.*, 11 January 1868. The *Ballarat Star* interpretation, 4 February 1867.

14 Lord's decision: personal communication from Miss D. Rait Kerr, 15 November 1966. The match is described in *The Times*, 13 June 1868; finance is recorded in Graham, Accounts, 15.

15 *Wisden: The Cricketers' Almanack for the Year 1869* (London, 1869), 12, 118–19, 155.

16 W. G. Grace and the Aborigines: '*W.G.*': *Cricketing Reminiscences* (London, 1899), 33. The ovation for Cuzens: *Nottingham Guardian*, 5 August 1868.

17 Twopenny's 'niner': *Sheffield Telegraph*, 12 August 1868; praise of Bullocky: *Brighton Gazette*, 11 June 1868. Critical commentators: *Yorkshire Gazette and Herald*, 18 July 1868; *The Times*, 27 May and 13 June 1868; 'Longstop', *Aust.*, 17 February 1869. Aboriginal prizes: *Sporting Life*, 21 October 1868; Red Cap: H. Heaton, *Dictionary of Dates and Men of the Time* (Sydney, 1879), part 2, 1. The watch awarded to Mullagh at Brighton on 9 June 1868 is with the Lawrence collection. It is inscribed 'presented to J. Mullagh by the gentlemen of Sussex for his fine display at Brighton'.

18 Unorthodox field placement: *Bury Times*, 25 July 1868.

19 Hove: *Brighton Gazette*, 11 June 1868.

20 Mullagh's performances were singled out for comment in almost every newspaper report on each match. Tarrant verdict: *Aust.*, 13 January 1900. His obituary is in *H.S.*, 15 August 1891.

6

Brighter Cricket

The Aborigines were the greatest exponents of brighter cricket in the history of the game. Although their methods were unorthodox, unlike contemporary cricket they did not rely upon electronic gadgetry for artificial effect, but devised their own special methods. Upon taking the field, they normally put the birds to flight with three rousing cheers and a strident whoop of encouragement for their opposition. Cricketing costume had not yet achieved the drab purity of modern fashion, but even by Victorian standards the Aborigines sported more colour than any team. Even more striking was their ensemble of possum skin and lyre-bird feathers worn during exhibitions of native skills. This was the same costume which they had worn in Sydney on the occasion of their farewell appearance, for which the feathers cost five pounds. Perhaps it appealed to those who hankered after the romantic life of the carefree savage. One spectator who saw them at the Oval believed that 'with a piece of fur wrapped round their loins and a sort of fur cap on their heads, they walked with a proud, elastic step that contrasted strangely with their former gait'. Another onlooker expressed his emotions in doggerel verse:

> *Arrayed in skin of kangaroo,*
> *And deck'd with lanky feather,*
> *How well you fling the fragile spear*
> *Along the Surrey heather.*

In his old age, Frank Gerald recounted something of his

youthful excitement as he watched five of the Aboriginal matches. Gerald's uncle had just returned from the Victorian gold-fields, sufficiently affluent to take his schoolboy nephew to see the opening game at the Oval. They travelled in a wagonette, supplied with a large hamper and liquid refreshments. As in all the matches which he saw, the Aborigines 'gave a good entertainment and the game was never slow'. They ran barefooted between the wickets, and in their enthusiasm they were 'heard as well as seen. They tore up and down the pitch, screaming and shouting native backchat'.

Gerald recalled that it was usual at the luncheon adjournment for the Aborigines to mix freely with the spectators, who supplied them liberally with 'cakes, biscuits and sweets and sometimes a drink out of a flask'. However, he noted that the management maintained strict control and beverages were limited to dilute sherry or tea. But Gerald's most vivid memory was of the first adjournment at the Oval. Perhaps his uncle deserves to go down to posterity as the initiator of Australian barracking at an English cricket ground. At the interval, his colonial uncle 'gave a loud "coo-ee!" and the players came running over to us. Then he talked to them in their own "patter" and soon they were jabbering round the wagonette like monkeys'.

Other expatriate Australians in England were also drawn to see their fellow countrymen. Mrs Mary Alsop drove her two children in their brougham to the Derby ground on 3 September to see the Aborigines lose their match: 'they did not play very well,' she observed with disappointment. Samuel Winter, from Murndal station, western Victoria, was at Lord's ground in June to watch the Aborigines play the MCC[1].

Advertisements for their matches are vintage Victoriana. Rochdale readers were enticed by the dual attractions of 'these coloured handlers of the willow' and the presence of the Healey Hall Brass Band to celebrate the first match played on the new ground behind the Bowling Green Inn. For sixpence admittance the spectator on the third day of the Trent Bridge match could listen to the Nottingham Sax-Tuba Band while watching cricket from 11 a.m. until 4 p.m. and thereafter witness the following 'Australian and English sports': 1. 100 yards flat races; 2. Running high jump; 3. Standing high jump; 4. 150 yards hurdle race; 5. Vaulting with poles; 6. Throwing the cricket ball; 7. 100 yards backwards; 8. Water bucket race; 9. Throwing the boomerangs, and spears, and kangaroo rats, by the Blacks; 10. Lawrence's feat with the bat and ball; 11. Dick Dick dodging the cricket ball.

Anyone wishing to enter for one of the first eight events had to pay an entrance fee of one shilling, but amateurs only need apply. For people of quality the entrance ground charge of one shilling permitted access to the better accommodation on the eastern side of the ground where 'a spacious marquee' awaited the ladies, and for half a crown patrons could park their carriages. Unfortunately there were no entrants for the water bucket race (Figure D).

The death of King Cole during June served to inspire another variant of extravagant Victorian sentiment. The following verses were printed as an *In memoriam* to King Cole[2]:

> *To Britain he came from the land of the West*
> *As a stranger for honour and glory,*
> *And now as a hero intrepid and bold*
> *Will his name be recorded in story.*

> *For not with the sword did he covet renown,*
> *The battle he fought was at cricket,*
> *In lieu of grim weapons of warfare he strove*
> *With the bat and the ball at the wicket.*

> *Still fortune was faithless and fickle to him,*
> *Not long in the strife he contended,*
> *And never did victory gladden his side,*
> *Whenever the fort he defended.*

Now run out for naught in the innings of life,
By the grave of the good is he sleeping;
Yet sad are his comrades though reckon they well
How safe is their mate in our keeping.

At these combined athletic and weapon-hurling exhibitions the Aborigines displayed considerable versatility, although some were specialists at certain feats. The most impressive group activity was a mock battle, involving six or more men. At Nottingham three Aborigines standing some 80 metres distant from three other spearmen were 'completely hedged in' by accurately thrown spears; the effect was made more dramatic by war-whoops. At the Oval, J. G. Wood estimated their distance apart as 75 to 85 metres, and he noted that on most occasions the aim was so deadly that unless the recipient had dodged aside he would have been struck by the spear. These spears and the wooden spear-throwers which propelled them were traditional weapons of the Western District people. The spears measured some two metres in length, the shaft consisting of hard wood, with a tip of reed about 30 centimetres long. Lieutenant-General Pitt-Rivers was attracted to the Oval by these spear-throwing exhibitions. A Crimean War officer and a student of the history of warfare, he was preparing his influential essays on the evolution of technology. He watched closely as spears were cast 100 metres with the assistance of wooden spear throwers, but he could not vouch for their accuracy. However, at Rochdale throws were definitely on target. It was stated that Dick-a-Dick hurled a spear for 130 metres at the Bootle ground.

Charley Dumas was the star boomerang thrower but he was ably assisted in this by Mullagh. Sundown also must have made the voyage chiefly on account of his expertise in this field. Pitt-Rivers commended the masterly skill of the throwers and used his observations to support a detailed study of the evolution of throwing-sticks among primitive societies. Most spectators, however, were totally unfamiliar with boomerangs and newspapers devoted much copy to their remarkable properties and the skill of Dumas and Mullagh in throwing them. Lancastrian wit prompted the *Rochdale Observer* to note that the boomerang 'is the nearest approach to Paddy's description of the gun that would shoot round a corner'. Yet it was a hazardous sport for the spectators. A stray dog was almost cut in two at the Oval and Wood saw a brass spur struck off the heel of an incautious spectator who moved across the boomerang's line of flight. There were windy days when this event was cancelled as a safety precaution. However, one windy Saturday at Bootle, when the crowd insisted on the exhibition despite Mullagh's expressed doubts, his boomerang drifted and struck a spectator, slicing his hat and lacerating his face, although not as seriously as the papers suggested. There was a doctor in the crowd to treat the injured man and the doctor requested the offending boomerang as his payment. There was a similar accident at Rochdale. Fortunately, a doctor pronounced that Master Wallace Leach had received a superficial wound, presumably because he was protected by his straw hat. There was another accident in Surrey, according to Lawrence, when yet another hat was damaged. The injured party 'came to me very frightened and threatening us with an action as his life had been in danger. I knew what he wanted and gave him the price of a new [hat and] he went away quite satisfied as the injured one was very old'.

Following the Bootle accident in September, the team management prudently publicized the need for care. The local paper commented prior to their Hove match that 'the Australians...caution the spectators to keep well upon the limits of the ground'. The first routine of throwing balls at Dick-a-Dick was hastily abandoned at the Oval when unruly 'roughs' intervened. However, during the 1860s, problems of crowd control were general in English and Australian sport. With thousands attending fixtures where the sports arena was demarcated only by ropes, or not at all, it was difficult to maintain safe boundaries. At athletic meetings runners frequently were obstructed during events or mobbed at their conclusion.[3]

Although modern cricketers might wish for an armoury of boomerangs with which to silence persistent barrackers, even with the Aborigines, such 'blood sports' were exceptional. Throwing the 'kangaroo-rat' was no exception. The name is misleading. Normally termed a 'weet-weet', this weapon consisted of a solid wooden or bone knob on a flexible handle about 60 centimetres in length. It was normally used for bringing down birds or small animals. After it had been swung rapidly backwards and forwards to gather momentum and flex the weapon, it was skimmed low along the ground with an underarm jerky motion. In an impressive display at the Oval one was hurled right across the arena.

Lawrence perfected his own routine, which drew gasps from the ladies and doubtless gained him the respect of his men. A cricket ball was thrown hard and high in his direction from across the field, and he invariably caught and balanced it on the blade of his bat. He repeated the performance by hitting the ball into the air a few times, on each descent it came to rest upon the bat's blade. During the tour another individual act was developed but, as the press referred to it on only two occasions, it may have proved less of a drawcard. The sources are in conflict as to whether credit for the initiative belongs to Peter or Charley Dumas. It was said to be Charley, who entertained at Hastings, during June. His whip cracked, 'with almost sleight-of-hand activity'. In Sheffield several weeks later, 'Peter (we believe)...gave an exhibition with the whip, and we never saw anyone who could make it "talk" like him. He afterwards whipped a sixpence off "Whittams" finger, but so lightly that it was hit twice before it dropped to the ground'.

Half a century later, William Shepherd attributed the stock whip act to the dextrous Mosquito, whose thong was said to be longer than five metres. In Shepherd's version, the event was a luncheon adjournment diversion in which he also participated. With an arm outstretched, Shepherd held a shilling lightly in his finger tips, while Mosquito deftly removed it with a lash. After repeating this feat two or three times, Mosquito pocketed the money, while onlookers clamoured to supply Shepherd with further silver. Always willing to please, Mosquito cracked his way to riches, whereupon Shepherd cannily retrieved his lead-off shilling. As a variation, on windless days Shepherd held a cigar or a clay pipe in his mouth and, fortunately, he never suffered any mishap. Shepherd delighted in the discomfiture of a rude, persistent score-card seller at Manchester. This extrovert insisted on holding the pipe in his own mouth. As his manner evidently annoyed Mosquito, the whip 'cut the tip off [his nose] as clean as if done with a razor'.[4]

Another basic attraction was the contest of throwing the cricket ball, a common form of challenge at that period. There are several records of Charley Dumas, Bullocky and Red Cap throwing just in excess of 100 yards. Dick-a-Dick was the outstanding competitor, throwing 104 yards at Bootle, 107 at Rochdale, 108 at Sheffield and 113 yards at Plymouth. These men proved capable of defeating local challengers, although on the day they were outdistanced at Nottingham by Hardstaff, an illustrious name at Trent Bridge, who threw the ball 102 yards. It is claimed by the historians of Surrey cricket that W. G. Grace demonstrated his superiority over the Aborigines with successive throws of 116, 117 and 118 yards. This achievement may belong more to folklore of 'WG' than with the actualities of the 1868 season, for Grace makes no reference to it in his various autobiographical books.[5]

Despite his habitual slowness off the mark, Johnny Cuzens was a fast sprinter and he won many races. He competed barefoot until Shepherd took him to a Sheffield shoemaker who specialized in running pumps, and an improved performance was claimed. Such 100-yard sprints were supposed to be against amateur challengers only. Professionals naturally coveted the pound prize and, with the connivance of the managers, sometimes backed themselves to win. Confident in Cuzens's ability, Lawrence or Shepherd quietly accepted bets of up to two pounds. 'We always won,' recalled the ancient Shepherd. Their faith in his speed was climaxed at the Oval during the last engagement of the tour, when they accepted a larger wager. Although Cuzens again started late and then lost one of his crafted shoes a few yards on, he defeated prominent professional sprinters. He was rewarded with £10. One insight into his character was provided by South Norton. Back in May, when Cuzens was ill, he was nursed in Norton's home.[6] Norton appreciated his gratitude and his 'cheerful, kindly disposition'.

Dick-a-Dick also was adept at running backwards and he invariably won or came second in that curious 100-yard event. He also participated in normal flat races and demonstrated his stamina at Nottingham when he won the 100-yard race, followed by a win in the 150-yard hurdle, even though he fell at the second hurdle. At Eastbourne, his natural action in the high jump was commented on because it contrasted with the 'rather clumsy manner' of the other Aborigines. (However, Mullagh, the best at high jumping, did not compete.) But his reputation chiefly rested upon his remarkable adaptation of a native practice to a European application. His crowd-pleasing act began when he stood in the arena grasping a narrow wooden parrying shield in his left hand (Plate 24). This was the standard Victorian defensive weapon. It averaged a metre in length, nine centimetres in width and was triangular in cross section, with a hand-grip carved out of the solid wood. A parrying shield weighed about one and a half kilograms and was decorated with deeply incised lines and other geometric designs. Dick-a-Dick protected the region of the hand-grip with a pad of possum skin. He held a curved wooden club, a single-combat weapon termed a 'leowell' or 'langeel', in his right hand. Dick-a-Dick challenged all-comers to stand 15 or 20 metres distant and pelt him with cricket balls. He protected his body and head with the shield and his legs with the club, used baseball-bat fashion to deflect the missiles. Pitt-Rivers saw him ward off balls thrown simultaneously and forcefully by three men, and Wood described 'a positive rain of cricket balls'. On one occasion in Australia 60 balls had been aimed at him. Wood felt astonished at the 'almost intuitive knowledge that he seemed to possess'.

Dick-a-Dick was a showman of whom Barnum would have been envious. It was not only what he achieved in the centre, but the manner in which he performed which delighted the crowds and converted his act into the dramatic closing scene. Reliving the action with the vivid memory of age, Lawrence described it in the present tense:

> the excitement becomes very great as Dick works himself forward and gets quite close to them and gives a yell which causes such a hearty response for Dick's novelty and pluck that they cheer him immensely.

On 25 August 1868, Dick-a-Dick's act was described in similar vein at Middlesborough: 'a laughable display of mingled daring and dexterity...who allowed any number to (singly) throw cricket balls from any distance over a dozen yards...defending himself...or simply dodging the balls. The impudent assurance with which he challenged the most skilful throwers and the grotesque grins and antics with which he greeted their inevitable failures to hit him, provoked the greatest mirth'. He delighted the Lincoln crowd when he 'merrily grinned at his opponents'.

Because his act became such a feature, journalists emphasized his habitual evasions; Lawrence claimed that he was never struck. In fact, although some hundreds of balls were aimed at him, there are records of only two direct hits in all the available reports. His second failure was at Eastbourne, in October, when he was struck on the foot. His first lapse was announced proudly a month previously, in the *Lincoln Standard*. It occurred at Derby, during the 31st engagement of the tour. 'It was asserted that he had not been hit by any thrower in England...very shortly afterwards S. Richardson threw a ball at him, and succeeded in hitting him on the left shoulder.' It is appropriate that the wooden club which Dick-a-Dick wielded so effectively is preserved in the Lord's cricket museum (Plate 29). It is unlikely that the caption is correct in describing the incised, knobbed end as replicating a rattlesnake's tail!

Dick-a-Dick continued to dodge balls with such 'grace and dexterity' (to borrow *Bury Times* phraseology) that the tour management began to reward him, although their motives are unknown. Graham's accounting entries, beginning with July, frequently credit payment of one pound or 10 shillings for 'Dick's dodging'. The spectators at Lewisham presented him with 50 shillings because of their satisfaction with his efforts. He soon was parted from his earnings. Shepherd recalled Dick-a-Dick's antics with some amusement and dubbed him 'a most eccentric individual'. It would have been kinder to call him a generous extrovert. At Swansea, for example, he spent almost £5 at the fun fair 'wheel of fortune'. It spun so successfully that he won numerous prizes which he gave to his friends. He kept the cheap Swiss clock, however, and Shepherd had the daily task of winding it. Dick-a-Dick became so attached to the clock that he was 'thoroughly enraptured...he carried this...under his arm everywhere during the remainder of the tour'. On departing from Dewsbury one morning, he forgot his clock until he reached the railway station. Despite Lawrence's frantic attempts to stop him, he hurried back to their hotel. A breathless Dick-a-Dick returned, clutching his beloved clock, to find that fortune again favoured him for the train was late. When the team sailed for home, Shepherd received the clock as a parting gift.

On another occasion, Dick-a-Dick returned from a bazaar

with sundry watches, chains, rings and scarf pins, which he handed around freely. He bore these garish trinkets on a picture the size of a door — yet another prize. At a loss to know what to do with the vast picture, he accepted Shepherd's advice that he raffle it for half a crown a ticket. Enriched by 30 shillings, he rid himself of the problem. 'He had no appreciation of art,' observed the helpful Shepherd.

When the team entertained the press at 'a sumptuous collation' at Maidstone's Railway Hotel, to mark the tour's end, it is not surprising that it was Dick-a-Dick who replied to the toast on behalf of the Aborigines. Sadly, these are the only words spoken on the tour which may be attributed to him. He stood up, and 'laconically...responded in a single sentence, "We thank you from our hearts", and sat down amidst loud applause'. His tour record should not end with that speech, however, but with an incident in the match at Burton-on-Trent, famed for its breweries. The Aborigines won easily, but that is not the point. Dick-a-Dick scored 12 runs in his first innings. Although he made only a single run in his second appearance at the crease, his dismissal has illustrious associations with the history of English brewing.[7] His scorecard reads 'caught Worthington, bowled Bass, 1'. The close connection between the brewing industry and professional cricket was illustrated further in an unusual manner. When the team played its last match at the Oval, all schoolchildren enrolled at the Licensed Victuallers' Schools were admitted free to witness the sports.[8]

Four of the weary team, Bullocky, Peter, Tiger and Twopenny, boarded the 1100-ton vessel *Dunbar Castle* at Gravesend on 19 October, two days after their farewell appearance at the Oval. The remainder left Paddington station by train for what was said to be a brief holiday in Devon. By returning to the scene of his birth, Hayman may have wished to bask in the reflected glory of his exotic colonial charges. He also expected to profit from a sports meeting staged in Plymouth on 19 October. He reckoned without the weather, for a strong cold wind kept the crowds at home, although at least four Royal Navy captains were present. As only £15.17.6 was collected at the gate, the Devon excursion cost the sponsors £74.15.8. The venture substantiates doubts concerning Hayman's business acumen. This was the only occasion on the tour under his direct control, for he was unaccompanied by Lawrence, Smith or Graham. Except for the match against the press, which the management staged as a goodwill gesture, but which rain ruined, no engagement on the tour proved so costly as this last fixture.

The sportsmen boarded the *Dunbar Castle* a week later, when it called at Plymouth. The fact that four of the team missed the Devon excursion highlights the important role played by the others during the tour in providing the mainstay of the field sports. Bullocky and Twopenny certainly justified their inclusion as cricketers, although Peter and Tiger also contributed little in that department.

To have entrusted Hayman with the sole care of Bullocky and Tiger also may have proved too risky. As discussed later, they were prone to drink heavily when the chance arose. Possibly Twopenny also proved difficult to control on long journeys. F. M. Harpur, who saw Twopenny practising in the Sydney Domain in 1870 and who seems to have had an affinity for colourful anecdotes, would have thought that he was. According to him, Twopenny always arrived late at railway stations on the tour, and he normally arrived 'with only one leg to his pants'.

George Smith also boarded the ship at Gravesend. He took the opportunity of taking home some stallion bloodstock. Graham remained in England, but Smith, Lawrence and his daughter travelled as cabin passengers, while the 10 Aborigines had intermediate berths. On 4 February 1869 the *Dunbar Castle* docked at Sydney. With the exception of unfortunate King Cole, the team was back on Australian soil exactly a year after its departure from Sydney.[9]

NOTES

[1] The romantic spectator was a student of ethnography, J. G. Wood, *The Natural History of Man* (London, 1880), vol 2, 3; the romantic versifier was quoted in C. Box, *The English Game of Cricket* (London, 1877), 327. For F. Gerald's account, see *A Millionaire in Memories* (London, 1936), 211–12. For Mrs Alsop's Derby attendance we are indebted to a personal communication from Dr C. C. Macknight, Canberra; for Samuel Winter, another personal communication from the late Miss Margaret Kiddle, Melbourne.

[2] Vintage advertising is represented in *Roch. Obs.*, 27 June 1868 and *Nottingham Guardian*, 5 August 1868. 'King Cole – In Memorium' was reprinted in *Cricket Scores and Biographies*, vol 10, 413–4. There were nine verses, but the first four suffice here to indicate its literary level.

[3] The spear-throwing exhibition was described by Wood, *Natural History*, vol 2, 44 and *Nottingham Guardian*, 5 August 1868. Pitt-Rivers's observations are included in J. L. Myres (ed), *The Evolution of Culture and Other Essays* (Oxford, 1906), 125. The Rochdale occasion is in *Roch. Obs.*, 4 July 1868. Dick-a-Dick's long throw at Bootle: Graham, Accounts, 42. Boomerang throwing: Myres, *Evolution of Culture*, 133–7; Wood, *Natural History*, vol 2, 49. Accidents: Bootle — *The Field*, 19 September 1868; *Liverpool Echo*, 22 August 1963; Lawrence MS no 3; *Scores and Biographies*, vol 10, 640 exaggerates injury. Rochdale: Graham, Accounts, 25. Threat of law suit: Lawrence MS no 3. Brighton warning: Graham, Accounts, 72. Lack of crowd control: B. Haley, *The Healthy Body and Victorian Culture* (Harvard, 1978), 130.

[4] The 'weet-weet' exhibition was witnessed by Wood, *Natural History*, vol 2, 41–2. The best description of this artefact and of others used by the team is in R. Brough Smyth, *The Aborigines of Victoria* (Melbourne, 1878), 2 vols. Whip exhibitions: Graham, Accounts, 20; *Sheffield Independent*, 13 August 1868; W. Shepherd, in W. R. Weir (ed), *Ayre's Cricket Companion* (London, 1919), 131.

[5] Throwing the cricket ball records of distance are, of course, only as reliable as the measurements made. The main sources are *Roch. Obs*, 4 July 1868; *Nottingham Guardian*, 5 August 1868. Graham, Accounts, 20, 42, 48; *Western Morning News* (Plymouth), 20 October 1868. At Hastings, Bullocky threw 107 yards and Charley Dumas 104 yards. The claim about W. G. Grace: Lord Alverstone and C. W. Alcock, *Surrey Cricket* (London, 1904), 398; A. G. Moyes, *Australian Cricket: A History* (Sydney, 1959), 155.

[6] Cuzens as sprinter: Shepherd, *Ayre's Cricket Companion*, 132–3; W. S. Norton, in Harris, *History of Kent Cricket*, 64.

[7] Dick-a-Dick's sports record is based upon *Nottingham Guardian*, 6 August 1868; *Eastbourne Standard*, 6 October 1868; Lawrence, MS 1, p 68; Middlesborough — Graham, Accounts, 55; *Lincoln Standard*, 8 September 1868; 'grace and dexterity' — *Bury Times*, 25 July 1868; his prizes: Shepherd, 131–2; his speech — *South Eastern Gazette*, 8 October 1868; Bass and Worthington — Graham, Accounts, 66.

[8] Schoolchildren spectators: *Daily Telegraph*, 16 October 1868. Other metropolitan schools also could gain free admittance for their pupils, but only after application to the Surrey Club. Children from parish schools were admitted to the previous game at Godalming — *Daily News*, 15 October 1868.

[9] Departure from England and the Plymouth interlude: *Sporting Life*, 21 October 1868; *Western Morning*, 20 October 1868. Twopenny: F. M. Harpur, 'Cricket Footprints on the Sands of Time' (1932), unpublished MS notebooks, State Library of Victoria, La Trobe Library, Private Collections, Box 305/1, vol 1.

7

Financial Gain, Human Cost

The Aboriginal cricket tour cannot be dismissed as a mere speculation or a stunt. Cricketing standards in both countries were at a fairly elementary level in 1868 and the better team members stand comparison with contemporary English players of calibre. Most team members were weak, but the score sheets prove that the majority of players who opposed them were little better. The effective strength of the team for most of the tour was precisely 11 men, and yet they presented themselves for every match as arranged. Shepherd also played with the team, normally when Lawrence rested. Only two other reserves were called upon. At Newcastle, Mullagh's name was entered in the score book but it was subsequently deleted when he became ill on the day of the match. In the emergency a local worthy and Tynemouth club benefactor, G. Shum-Storey, took his place.[1] The other occasional player was Hayman's kinsman, W. S. Norton. Norton captained the team at Hastings on 22–23 June. It was stated that Lawrence had injured his hand, but a possible explanation for Lawrence's absence was the death in a London hospital of King Cole on 24 June.

It must be concluded that both team and management made a conscientious attempt to play the game. Their reliability and their many feats of quickness of eye and dexterity prove that they had not succumbed unduly to the temptations of alcohol. There were also English precedents for some of the more colourful features of the tour. All-England XIs had dressed in distinctive manner and had competed in athletics meetings while on tour. Of course, the

Aborigines added what were termed 'native sports' to the programme. It is interesting that no writers criticized these activities, and the impression conveyed by all of them is that the Aborigines gave good and exciting value. There was sufficient scientific interest in their display to bring Pitt-Rivers and Wood to the Oval, both of them interested in different aspects of the evolution of material culture. Contrary to original expectations, these two were the only eminent men concerned with evolutionary theory who commented on the appearance and achievements of the Aboriginal visitors. It would prove simple to name an XI consisting of Darwinian evolutionary theorists who should have found the Aborigines worth watching.

English spectators received the Aboriginal team enthusiastically and without indications of displeasure at the standard of cricket; the novelty and professionalism of 'native sports' met with universal acclaim. Attendance figures calculated before the use of turnstiles may be elastic, although on those few instances where newspapers cite them, the numbers accord reasonably with the crowd which might have been expected from the total gate receipts. There were 7000 at the Oval for the tour opening, but this followed a flurry of publicity. On the first day at Sheffield, the crowd numbered around 5000; the team's first victory was witnessed at Lewisham by 4000. Keighley attracted 3500 patrons, while 3000 attended at Swansea, and a similar number paid the shilling admittance to see the third (sports) day at Hastings. There were between 2300 and 3000 people at each of the three days of the Hove game, the Lord's attracted a crowd of 3000 on the first day, while the crowd at Hastings rose from 500 on the opening day to more than 3000 on the sports day. Attendance at a number of fixtures, including the popular Sheffield match, the game at Scarborough seaside resort and the team's farewell game at the Oval, were affected by bad weather. As the tour was profitable during its first 12 weeks, but its profitability dropped by almost two-thirds during its second half, the promoters were rash to continue the season so far into October. During the final weeks they contended with deteriorating weather and declining popular interest due to over-exposure of the team. The gate takings indicate that the staging of return matches at the same ground was poor business (see Appendix V).

The team made losses on eight fixtures, the first being the 23rd match. The financial loss amounted to £186.6.7. Three of these unprofitable engagements were return matches, while £161 of this amount was accounted for by the 'goodwill' match against the press and by Hayman's foolhardy excursion to Plymouth.

Unlike the All-English XI visits to Australia, where gold dust evidently powdered the wickets, no fortunes awaited the eager colonial cricketer in England. Conflicting opinions have been expressed concerning the profitability of the Aboriginal tour. Shepherd claimed that Graham showed him the balance sheet, which indicated a loss of £2000, and Lawrence asserted a similar loss by the management. Analysis of Graham's ledger refutes such pessimism, because although not a financial bonanza, it more than covered its costs. Total receipts in England amounted to £5416, while costs amounted to £3224. Against this gross surplus of £2192, Graham's subsidy in Australia must be debited. Accordingly, a surplus of £1008 appears possible, or around £1100 when some double counting in respect of advances to Hayman are taken into account.

On the other hand, even though expenses were covered, there is no indication that Lawrence, Hayman or Smith received any payments above such allowances. As Graham evidently was the investor, he presumably retained the surplus. Certainly, although the management enjoyed a return visit home to England, they did not take back fortunes to the colonies.

Were the players paid? The Aborigines voyaged both ways under conditions superior to that of most migrants, while the condition of their accommodation and their general welfare throughout an 18-month absence from their territory were reasonable. They picked up prize money fairly regularly at the field sports and Mullagh, Cuzens and Dick-a-Dick, at least, probably collected amounts far in excess of a Western District rural labourer's wage. Given the ethos of Aboriginal society, all these bonuses would have been shared among the team.

The management may have let it be thought that the players received regular wages, but there is no evidence that they did. Only days before the team sailed for home, the *Eastbourne Gazette* felt positive that a bonus would be paid:

> We believe we are justified in saying that besides their weekly wages, and ordinary expenses allowed them in England, they will each receive £50 upon their return home.

Graham closed his accounts with an entry on 9 October, two days after the Eastbourne newspaper's prediction. As he did not voyage home with the team, any bonus paid to them in Australia could not be recorded in his book. It must be observed, however, that if each Aborigine received £50, it would have drained all available funds. Despite this apparent lack of wages, however, given working conditions at that time, it cannot be claimed that they were unduly exploited.

Because of the prestige of *Cricket Scores and Biographies*, cricket historians sometimes accept assertions printed therein without question. Such an author was C. H. B. Pridham, in his popular book on *The Charm of Cricket Past and Present*. Following the above source, he stated that business arrangements for tour fixtures took one of two forms. Either the team received a payment of £200 outright for their appearance, or they collected all the gate money, paid the expenses of staging the match, and gave £20 to the local club concerned. He cited the Swansea match as an example of the latter form of arrangement. Graham's accounts for the Swansea fixture confirm that the club indeed received £20 and that the Aboriginal team paid all costs and retained the balance, thereby making £43 profit. It is erroneous, however, to generalize from that one known example to all matches. The arrangements almost always differed from those expounded by *Scores and Biographies*, and not once did the promoters receive £200, so that assertion is entirely misleading.

Some clubs agreed to have a game staged without any fee; more importantly, the publicans who arranged them were delighted to attract a thirsty crowd. At the other extreme was the MCC, which demanded 50 per cent of gross receipts at Lord's, but apparently met all the costs of staging the match. The Oval required one-quarter of receipts for the first match, but secretary Burrup accepted less than one-fifth for the return game. Major grounds such as Trent Bridge, Sheffield and Bootle negotiated for one-fifth, the same percentage as paid to Julius Caesar for arranging the obscure challenge against XI Gentlemen of Godalming. The popular Hove encounter against the Sussex club was arranged for only a £10 fee; as the profit was £168, the tourists were fortunate. It is evident that the commercial circuit was a free enterprise system, but that the Aboriginal tourists received reasonable consideration from club managements.[2]

On the other hand, under such negotiations, the tour management was obliged to meet all expenses involved in staging matches. These included payment for gatemen, police at the ground and umpires at the wicket, publicity, team refreshments, sports prizes and, occasionally, brass bands. Behind all this expenditure was the cost of Mr 'five per cent' Hingston, the agent who arranged the mundane details above and who, during the course of the tour, earned £102.14.3. A general dissection of expenditure is provided in Table A, Appendix V.

Scores and Biographies and its derivatives contain further unco-ordinated details of this tour, but some are unverifiable. Anthropologists may boggle at the assertion that the Aborigines belonged to the 'Werrumbrook' tribe, certainly located accurately areawise between the Glenelg and Wimmera Rivers, but attributed to 'the real *Polynesian* species'. Such racial confusion is reminiscent of comment in *The Times*, 26 May 1868, whose readers were regaled with the information that the newly arrived cricketers 'represent the colonies of Victoria, Queentown, South Australia and New Zealand'.

Indeed, perhaps the tour literally coloured British concepts of Australian cricket. Sir Pelham Warner relates that when D. W. Gregory led the first white Australians to England in 1878 it caused embarrassment at Lord's.[3] A spectator who met a cricketer friend observed in conversational manner: 'So I hear you are going to play against the niggers on Monday.' Unfortunately, his friend was sitting with Spofforth, the star Australian bowler. He was introduced forthwith as 'the demon nigger bowler'.

If this incipient racism was a subject for humour in 1878, what was the English attitude to the Aborigines 10 years earlier? The anthropologist in search of racial tensions is impressed more by their rarity than with their serious nature. At least the newspapers featured positively the achievements of the visitors or reported genuinely humorous aspects of the games, rather than displaying overt racialism. No newspaper was found to use the term 'nigger'; when 'sable', 'dusky', 'blacks', or comparable terms were employed, it was not in the totally derogatory sense but in a facetious or patronizing manner. The sheer ignorance of local communities was a reality, but familiarity with the team soon bred comradeship rather than contempt.

Lawrence recounted such an experience, when the travel-weary tourists reached Brighton:

I thought to give the Blacks a bath before breakfast [and] took them...a great number of people following[.]

We could hear them saying they will never allow them in as the dye will spoil the Bath thinking they were white men and just dyed for the occasion[.] This idea so impressed the ticket clerk that he w'd [*sic*] not give tickets until he washed and rubbed them with towles [*sic*] this satisfied him and the people for they cheered them as they came out.

The publican of the Bat and Ball Inn at Gravesend, where the team was to board during its third English match, was concerned that his hotel would suffer from a visitation by savages. He applied to the local Board of Guardians 'to lend him a quantity of beds and bedding for the accommodation of the black cricketers'. His application was rejected. Graham pasted the newspaper clipping of the incident in his accounts ledger and wrote 'a Blackguard' against the piece. The fact that Graham highlighted the matter probably indicates its rarity. Possibly the publican still won his claim, because his accommodation bill for £40 was well above the average cost for board on the tour.

There was an unpleasant incident at York, when the Aborigines were excluded from the luncheon tent. The Aborigines were offended and Mullagh vowed that he would not take the field again. It is significant that it is the only incident of this type culled from various sources and that the local newspaper observed 'this untoward event was the cause of much criticism and many comments'. The club president later denied strenuously that any discrimination had occurred and he explained that Mullagh withdrew because of illness. It may be relevant to the frayed tempers that tactful Lawrence was absent and Shepherd was leading the team. Whatever the actual facts, the teams ate separately and the partisan crowd took the allegations seriously. 'That the sympathy of the public was with their darker brethren,' the *York Herald* observed, 'was unmistakeably visible on the second day by the enthusiasm which seemed to pervade them.' Fine sentiments which deplored racial discrimination also pervaded the press. As an inelegant versifier put it:

> Now Gents should be Gents and not snobs,
> But I am sorry to say,
> The Yorkists refused the Blacks to lunch,
> Until they done that day,
> In Australia our cricketers were treated well,
> And I'll be bound to say,
> Every honest heart will say so,
> In a handsome sort o' way.

The *York Herald* was more moralistic.[4] 'Cricket has hitherto owed much of its popularity as a national pastime,' it warned, 'to the perfect equality on which all who indulge in the game have met at the wickets, and it were a pity therefore that a breach of the good old custom should have taken place in the case of a team representing those under the same rule as ourselves at the antipodes.'

Such sentiments reflected prevailing social notions, so that in any assessment of the extent of racial tolerance experienced by the Aboriginal tourists, the influence of current social philosophy is a potent force. It has been observed of the growth of British racialism during the nineteenth century that, through popular revulsion from slavery, the initial response to black people in Britain was humanitarian. The American Civil War and its prelude made black people familiar figures in England, for whom sympathy was felt. They were accepted largely as individuals and judged according to their abilities to conform to British social conventions. Consequently, black, English-speaking, well-dressed and quiet-mannered cricketers were unlikely to be assigned too lowly a social status. In this context, however, they were just in time. With the rising popularity of scientific racialism, or social Darwinism, racial attitudes after the 1860s became more strident and stratified according to class. While earlier humanitarianism might proclaim the notion that all men were brothers, social Darwinism inferred that the Aboriginal race, in particular, was less equally endowed than others. That great pioneering anthropologist, Baldwin Spencer, was to write:[5]

Australia is the present home and refuge of creatures, often crude and quaint, that have elsewhere passed away and given place to higher forms. This applies equally to the Aboriginal as to the platypus and kangaroo. Just as the platypus laying its eggs and feebly suckling its young, reveals a mammal in the making, so does the Aboriginal show us what early man must have been like.

Another potent factor in the intellectual climate around mid-century was muscular Christianity which, in the British task of imperial assimilation and cultural uplift, added cricket to the invisible baggage constituting the white man's burden. 'Games conduce not merely to physical, but moral health,' proclaimed Henry Kingsley, the apostle of Christianity-through-sportsmen. In the distant Victorian colony, these sentiments were echoed by the editor of the *Ballarat Star*. In praising the work of converting black shearers into 'smart cricketers', it prophesied that 'the order of civilization in the Christian sense seems to be first to make savages men and then to make them Christians'. Many contemporary World Series Cricket heroes might scorn the stern advice proffered fictional schoolboy Tom Brown, nine years before the Aboriginal tour, that cricket bred unselfish boys, because 'it merges the individual in the eleven', and that one 'doesn't play that he may win, but that his side may'. Such concepts were intended also to promote the bonding of the rapidly changing English social orders.[6] Secure in both his status and his property, Lord William Pitt Lennox extolled cricket as a social leveller, although this did not imply for him any economic or political equality.[7]

'No game tends more to promote a good understanding between the upper ten thousand and the humbler classes,' he wrote, 'than the social intercourse which takes place during a game of cricket, when the peasant vies with the peer, the private soldier with the officer, the labourer with the landowner. In this truly national contest a nobleman's stumps may be lowered without any levelling system following such an event...In fact, there is no game which promotes health and recreation, good humour and social intercourse, more than cricket.'

It suited the interests of the newly enriched commercial and industrial classes to adapt to such cosy notions to combat tensions between employers and the swelling ranks of urban workers. So, also, aspiring and otherwise individualistic professional cricketers conformed to the whims of their club patrons and employers. Not only did they cut their cloth to measure, but when many of them walked onto the cricket field, their trousers were fastened by belts inscribed with the motto, 'The Prince and peasant by cricket are united'. The preface to Richard Daft's memoirs, written by Andrew Lang, is a relevant reminder of professional cricketing ambitions. Daft, the Nottinghamshire professional, had a brother who played against the Aborigines at Trent Bridge. Lang's words have a familiar ring.[8] 'Cricket is a very humanising game. It appeals to the emotions of local patriotism and pride. It is eminently unselfish...and binds all the brethren together, whatever their politics and rank may be.' *James Lillywhite's Cricket Annual* voiced similar sentiments in 1873, urging the virtues of 'unselfishness, humility and self-restraint'.[9] 'It is a great thing particularly in these days, that My Lord, and Sir John, and his Reverence should mix in terms of legitimate equality with the farmer, the blacksmith, and the butcher, whether as players or spectators.' The appearance of the Aborigines at Lord's, where they played against lords, conforms with these aristocratic notions and practices of cricket. The *York Herald* therefore voiced humane but orthodox opinion when it criticized the behaviour of the York Club.

More typical of English team attitudes was the Derby match, where the Boar's Head catered for players 'and every attention was afforded them'. At the conclusion of their final game at the Oval, the Surrey Club entertained the entire team at dinner. When the president of Bootle Club presented Mullagh with a purse, he was fulsome in his praise, claiming that there was no finer all-rounder in England. A lengthy report on their Keighley appearance was unstinting in its support, concluding that the Aborigines were 'men worth playing at cricket with'. The whimsical article on the Norwich match betrays no racism. The Aborigines were praised as 'square broad shouldered fellows, with their burly black faces and their beaming eyes, dashing about the field with. . .lithe suppleness. . .it was hard to realise the savage by some supposed to be the most degraded in creation beneath their gay scarlet shirts. . .However degraded or not, they defeated the Carrow Club in one innings'.

The frequent references to 'merry' fieldsmen and praise for their athleticism indicates that team spirit and enjoyment in the game remained generally high. Some sudden collapses may be explained by wet or cold weather affecting morale. What of life off the field? Graham's accounting entries show that hotel lodging bills always were paid and that the charges indicate that the European managers lived at about the same standard themselves. Similarly, the team voyaged home in the same comparative comfort of intermediate class, as on the outward voyage, and was not relegated to the steerage. It is likely that they normally shared accommodation, whereas the Europeans had separate rooms. However, such communal life would accord with Aboriginal preferences. Dick-a-Dick's farewell speech, and an improbable single sentence attributed to Twopenny, are the only comments traced to individuals; Lawrence normally passed any vote of thanks, even when Mullagh was the central figure, as when he received his purse at Bootle. In any conversations with press representatives they appeared polite but reticent, as is the Aboriginal characteristic today when in unfamiliar surroundings. The description of their reaction at Norwich is an understandable impression conveyed to a stranger — 'speaking English tolerably well...and treating anyone addressing them with a surly civility'.

Their leisure time must have been passed largely in trains or coaches moving rapidly from place to place. Some of their journeys must have been the result of poor planning. To travel to Bradford from Rochdale via Swansea makes as little sense as when they played at Burton-on-Trent, Liverpool and in Essex, in that order; from Bury they went to Norwich and back-tracked to Keighley (Figure E). However, most fixtures occurred over a more logical geographic spread which enabled some time for socializing. How they passed their evenings is beyond the record, except for one tantalizing entry in Graham's account book. While they were staying in Liverpool at the end of July, £3.0.6. is debited against 'Music Hall'.

Alcohol had spoiled the first tour with Wills as captain, and over-indulgence seemed to form one of the rules of cricket in those days. During the English tour it remained a problem, but one which the management attempted to control with considerable success. Only during the Sheffield match is there positive evidence that some of the players drank heavily. A report on the game praised the standard of play, but noted that one of the best players was unavailable. Bullocky was the culprit; 'a predilection for fire-water and a natural indolence are some of the troubles with which the managers have to contend'. Worse was to follow, for early the next morning Tiger mauled a policeman in King Street. Tiger was seen drunk and disorderly at 2 a.m., and he assaulted two policemen who approached him. 'He knocked one of them down and attempted to strangle him whilst on the ground.' During the scuffle 'Tiger got his head broke', and a doctor was called to dress his wound. In court next day, Tiger was threatened with prison, but was released with a caution and a one-pound fine. This was paid immediately by the cricket club secretary, who excused Tiger by stating that he had 'rather a weak mind'. 'It appears Tiger occupied the post of long slip,' the plausible secretary explained, but that 'he had given them the slip — (laughter) — as they were under the belief that he was at his lodgings at the time the assault was committed.' Despite his injury, Tiger took the field at Dewsbury two days later, top-scoring in the first innings with 20 runs, followed by 5 in the second innings. Bullocky did not join him in the team until the following match, whereupon he was run out for no score. As Bullocky failed to take the field between 28 July and 17 August, the indications are that he was suffering from a severe drinking problem.

When the team assembled at Burton-on-Trent to play the brewers, including Bass and Worthington, temptation must have scented the air. The local newspaper praised the team's behaviour, but added that, 'with one exception nothing was done by them to annoy their excellent captain'. Although the identity of this man and his misdemeanour are unknown, it is worth noting that both Tiger and Bullocky played in this and the succeeding match.

King Cole's death cannot be attributed to alcohol, because he was a regular and reasonable performer in the first eight matches and in Australia the previous season, until a week before his death. Pneumonia was the occasion, although his lungs may have been affected by tuberculosis. Even so, the management cannot be held responsible and there was no adverse press comment. Jim Crow also was a regular, if ineffective, team member until his last game on 13–15 August. Sundown, whom he accompanied back to Australia, is never mentioned in any records after his two meagre appearances. Neither is there any financial record concerning their passage home. An entry in Graham's ledger may provide a clue. Listed in the expenses for the match following Jim Crow's last game is the sum of £22.7.6, credited to 'secretary's account'. Such a large amount may represent their passage money on the *Parramatta*, under the care of their old friend Captain Williams. Sundown's health must have been poor from the start of the tour but the nature of his illness is not known.[10]

In the case of all the men, however, a significant psychological factor must have operated which partly may explain Sundown's dejection, or drinking outbursts by others. These Aborigines were removed suddenly from familiar traditional surroundings to a world beyond their wildest imaginings. 'Homesickness' can prove a traumatic experience for many people, but in the case of Aborigines, for whom identification with specific localities was vital, prolonged absence from place, kin and traditional obligations must have weighed heavily upon them. Listen to the wistful voice of their contemporary, Jackey White, whose country on the Wannon River lay to the south-east of their land. Jackey White wrote to S. P. Winter, of Murndal station, near Hamilton.[11] The year was 1877 and he resided on Lake Condah Mission Station, only 30 kilometres distant. He had been moved there by government order, acting under the misguided and arbitrary paternalism of the Board for the Protection of the Aborigines, whose policy was to congregate Aboriginal people at settlements, no matter where they originated.

'I want to come back to Wannon,' Jackey White cried, 'I knew you ever since I was a boy you used to keep us (a)live I recollect about thirteen or fourteen years ago when you used to travel about five or six miles to bring us to your place, so will you be obliged to write to the government for us and get us off here, I will do work for you and will never leave you — I always wish to be in my own country where I was born — I am now miserable, all the Wannon blackfellows are all dead and I am left — This country don't suit me I'm a stranger in this country I like to be in my country.' This sad man was only 30 kilometres, or a day's walk, from his familiar traditional lands; the cricketers were separated from their own territories by half the world and months on the ocean. Taking all this into account, it makes the Aboriginal tour all the more remarkable.

At some late period in his life, Charles Lawrence thought about the problems of his Aboriginal charges. He pinned three sheets of paper with his reflections into a notebook. One of these undated pages indicates the problems and tensions involving alcohol throughout the tour. It shows Lawrence as a man of sympathy and understanding, but it also highlights the realities of life as a roving commercial cricketer.[12] It is quoted in full, as written, at a time when the tour was a sentimental memory and probably all the Aborigines were dead:

...it had been most trying to keep them in order under the influence of alcohol which could not be kept from them as they were every day in touch with lovers of cricket who thought it kind to induce them to drink their health and chat with them until the poor fellows got quite helpless to refuse. When I remonstrated with this friendly treatment of the people they said they were not slaves and should have what they liked as they were in a free country and I must not stop them therefore taking all these things into consideration they behaved very obedient [sic] and did their best to help me and was always saying it was the gentlemens fault and would make them drink their health and like children would promise to be better I always forgave them after breakfast and said how sorry I was and that I should have to take them home again if they did not improve but I felt sure they would try but under the influence of drink it was hopeless for each disposion [sic] would develop one would quarrel and want to fight another would sulk others wd [sic] play games quite harmless and profess their love for me and would do anything to please me what ever else could I do than forgive them and hoping for improvement. I became their professor [*sic*] before we left Australia with my promise not to develop anything they wd. tell me this had a good effect.

NOTES

[1] For G. S. Storey, see Graham, *Accounts*, 52, 54.

[2] Payment to Aborigines: *Eastbourne Gazette*, 7 October 1868. A contemporary estimate that the investors broke even is provided by C. Box, *The English Game of Cricket* (London, 1877), 329. W. Shepherd, *Ayre's Cricket Companion*, 1919, 134. For a modern claim that £2000 was lost, see K. Dunstan, *The Paddock that Grew* (Melbourne, 1962), 34. The financial arrangements for matches: C. H. B. Pridham, *The Charm of Cricket Past and Present*, 27.

[3] The Spofforth story is told by P. F. Warner, *Lord's 1787–1945* (London, 1946), 59.

[4] The Brighton baths: Lawrence, MS 3; the Bat and Ball Inn: Graham, *Accounts*, 6; the Yorkshire incident was reported in the *Yorkshire Gazette*, 18 July 1868; *York Herald*, 18 July and 25 July 1868; the unlabelled poem is pasted in Graham, *Accounts*, 31.

[5] Cricket and social philosophy: D. A. Lorimer, *Colour, Class and the Victorians* (Leicester, 1978), 13–19, 67. W. B. Spencer and F. J. Gillen, *The Arunta* (London, 1927), preface.

[6] The quotations from Kingsley (1874) and *Tom Brown's Schooldays* (1857) are from Bruce Haley, *The Healthy Body and Victorian Culture* (Harvard, 1978), 119, 153; see also the interesting essay by K. A. P. Sandford, 'Cricket and Victorian society', *Journal of Social History* 17 (1983): 302–17. The *Ballarat Star* prophecy, 4 February 1867.

[7] Lord W. P. Lennox, *Sport at Home and Abroad* (London, 1872), 2 vols, vol 2, 8. Information concerning belt buckles: H. Cunningham, *Leisure in the Industrial Revolution c1780–c1880* (New York, 1980), 119.

[8] Richard Daft, *Kings of Cricket* (Bristol, [1893]), 12. See also W. F. Mandle, 'W. G. Grace as a Victorian hero', *Historical Studies*, 19 (1980).

[9] G. W. King, 'On the social and moral aspects of cricket', *James Lillywhite's Cricketers' Annual* (London, 1874), 24–5.

[10] Alcohol: Sheffield – *Aust.*, 21 November 1868, 652; unlabelled newspaper clippings in Graham, *Accounts*, 47–8; Burton-on-Trent — Graham, *Accounts*, 66. Sundown: *Aust.*, 19 December 1868, 780.

[11] Jackey White's letter is quoted in M. Kiddle, *Men of Yesterday* (Melbourne, 1961), 129.

[12] For comment upon the lifestyle of English professional cricketers and their tendency to drink heavily, see W. F. Mandle, 'The professional cricketers in English in the nineteenth century', *Labour History*, 23 (1972), 14.

8

After Stumps

Happily, the fears of the Victorian Board for the Protection of the Aborigines had not been realized. The team was not marooned in England and, except for the death of King Cole and the premature return of Sundown and Jim Crow, they arrived in Sydney apparently in good health on 4 February 1869. The prolonged and strenuous tour may be considered as exploitation of their physical resources, but there is no evidence to indicate that they were unhappy and Lawrence drove himself as hard as his men. There is certainly nothing to support the view that grog was used as an inducement to retain the services of the players, and their accomplishments are evidence to the contrary. It may be inferred, however, that they received no cash bonus upon their return home.

Before the team left Sydney for home, a match was organized at the Albert Ground. On 12 February, New South Wales were 5 wickets down for 51 runs when rain forced the abandonment of play. Torrential rains fell, causing serious washaways and flooding in Sydney, so that the team was dogged by bad weather in its belated attempts to increase funds.

Back in Melbourne on 18 February, there was apparently no need for subterfuge and concealment to escape the wrath of the Board for Protection of the Aborigines for their precipitate departure in 1867. Perhaps on the principle that nothing succeeds like success, the safe return of the tourists quashed all opposition from officials and humanitarians. There were no special board meetings called to discuss cricketing affairs and no one wrote letters of protest to the press.

The Melbourne Cricket Club readily made its ground available for a three-day match, beginning on 20 February, on the basis of 15 per cent gross receipts. This match was drawn, but the Aborigines gave a more polished display than in 1867, and it elicited favourable comment from former critics. 'Longstop' (W. J. Hammersley), who was forthright in his criticism before their departure, felt 'astonished' at their progress, especially in batting. The Victorian team possibly was the strongest combination which the Aborigines ever faced. It scored 237, to which the former coach of the Aborigines, Tom Wills, contributed 26 not out. Still recovering from their voyage from Sydney and with Cuzens and Peter ill, the Aborigines were fortunate to force a draw. They made 141, and at the close of play were 7 wickets down for 100 in their second innings. Twopenny scored 32 and Mullagh 31. After stumps were drawn Dick-a-Dick gave his habitual exhibition of dodging cricket balls. He maintained his equanimity despite the climatic vagaries, which witnessed century temperatures on the opening day and cold winds and hail on the last.

They played a final game in Melbourne and in the stratified colonial society of that day it must be designated a social triumph. The itinerant Duke of Edinburgh was back in town and his activities still dominated press headlines as they had done two years before. It was announced that on 2 March the Aborigines would play a combined team of the officers of HMS *Galatea* and the military garrison. The duke was there, and so was the naval band from his ship. Proceeds were donated to the Aborigines, but unfortunately it was the hot weather which restricted attendance on this occasion. It proved a high-scoring game, perhaps the greatest feast of run-making with which the Aborigines were associated, and almost certainly their highest score. They closed their innings with 9 wickets down for 331 runs, of which Lawrence made 68, Cuzens 63, Twopenny 56, Red Cap 36, Mullagh 27 and Bullocky 28. Tiger and Peter maintained their accustomed form, however, and both failed to score. In reply, the officers scored 293 for the loss of 5 wickets, three of them falling to Mullagh, and two to Bullocky, who had bagged only twice that number during his entire English tour. Like their exit from the colony 17 months earlier, this splendid climax to their tour before their return to their lands has been unrecorded by historians of cricket during the past century.[1]

Most of the cricketers departed from Melbourne for obscurity and premature death. They were reported in Hamilton on 10 March, where they gave a brief exhibition of their skills, but a proposed match fell through, whereupon they dispersed to their homes. Five days later the energetic Cuzens represented his Balmoral club in a game against Harrow. Before relapsing into a long silence on the topic of Aboriginal cricketers, the *Hamilton Spectator* paid a glowing tribute to Hayman and his team. It is possible, however, that credit for his 'excellent generalship' was due as much to Lawrence and Smith, both now returned to Sydney. 'The appearance of the darkies is, in every way, creditable to themselves and to Mr. Hayman,' pronounced the paper, 'they seem to have undergone a process of civilisation which has changed their nature thoroughly, and their conduct would compare favourably with most white men.'

Regrettably, this unqualified and Eurocentric praise may have been premature. While the team was safely escorted home, it seems most unlikely that members received any substantial monetary reward for their 'stalwart' service. At the time of their departure from England, no payments were recorded in Graham's ledger. Before their first Melbourne appearance, the now sympathetic *Australasian* hoped for a large crowd at the MCC, in order to provide the players with funds, it being 'well known that the speculation...has barely paid expenses'. There was also the case of the enigmatic Sundown and his fellow-traveller Jim Crow. There is one clue to the nature of their homecoming, which if substantiated, would reflect badly upon the team management. In December 1868, four months after Sundown sailed from England, the *Hamilton Spectator* carried an ominous news item. 'Sundown penniless and broken in health was set down in the courtyard of the Victoria Hotel by a generous Cobb and Co. coachman, who had brought him to Hamilton "gratis"... a victim of neglect, rather than the hero of black cricketing speculators.'

The *Australasian* rallied immediately to the defence of the team's management, pointing out that the men had returned on the familiar *Parramatta*. (If the ship still was under the command of Captain Wiliams, the two men would have been certain of a caring voyage.) Once arrived in Sydney, the newspaper assured its readers, Sundown was put on the Melbourne steamer and was provided later with transport to Hamilton. (Jim Crow is not mentioned in this item.) Arrangements were in hand for him to board the Cobb and Co. coach for Edenhope. Possibly excited to be within familiar territory at last, he disregarded travel instructions, and Sun-down 'shouldered his carpet bag and walked off home', presumably into the sunset.[2]

European interest in the team had evaporated. Only in 1891 was it newsworthy again, at the time of Mullagh's death. During a period of deep nostalgia, old-timers recalled the team's origins through letters to the *Hamilton Spectator*. Hayman wrote to record his belief that only Red Cap and the resilient Tarpot were alive.[3]

The team's exploits proved a more lasting stimulus to Aboriginal people. For the next three decades cricket was played with verve by Aborigines from Queensland to Western Australia (Plate 35). Some of these activities were outlined in the opening chapter. Unfortunately, the return of the team to their traditional territories coincided with times when welfare policies of the Board for the Protection of the Aborigines, in conjunction with missions, were being implemented. They were to determine the future lives of several cricketers. Officials preferred to concentrate Aborigines on reserves, where it was believed that more efficient control and instruction would improve their social and spiritual condition. This ran counter to the Aboriginal preference for familiar territories and meant that people from many and diverse backgrounds played cricket on grounds which must have seemed almost as foreign as those trodden by the adventurous 1868 team.

In 1858 the Moravian missionaries had established the Ebenezer station at Antwerp, north of Horsham and near Lake Hindmarsh, as a centre for Wimmera Aborigines. The Framlingham Aboriginal station, near Warrnambool, was formed in 1861 but it was only firmly established under board direction in 1869. In this same year Lake Condah station, near Hamilton, was founded on a working basis by the Church of England Mission Committee. There was another small reserve at Dergholm, on the Glenelg River, north-west of Casterton, and another at Colac, on the road to Geelong. The centre which was most visited by Europeans was the government station established at Coranderrk, north of Melbourne, near modern Healesville.

The diminutive but athletic Cuzens was employed at the Melbourne Cricket Ground, but his stay in Melbourne was a brief one. In October 1869, Hayman wrote to the Melbourne Cricket Club on behalf of Cuzens and Mullagh (Plate 31). Evidently, they were engaged for 20 weeks during the 1869–70 season at the rate of one pound each per week, their board and half their travelling expenses. Cuzens played in only six matches during the season, in eight innings only scoring 81 runs with the club's Second XI and taking 9 wickets for 71 runs from 192 balls. His vitality had deserted him and his engagement was terminated around mid-March. As he had insufficient funds to return home, some nine pounds was paid by the MCC to assist him.

Possibly he was ailing. Upon his return to the Western District, where board regulations now applied, he resided at

Framlingham station, where he died on 22 March 1871. He had developed a cold several weeks previously. After an apparent recovery, he accompanied Mosquito to the Warrnambool Highland gathering. A soaking in the boisterous weather induced another cold which, aggravated by dysentery, proved fatal. A Warrnambool well-wisher notified his death to the Melbourne Cricket Club, requesting a financial contribution for a 'decent burial'. However, as the MCC evidently pleaded that 'club funds will not permit', Cuzens was given a public funeral by the police. In the presence of the Framlingham Community, he was buried at a service conducted by the station superintendent.

However, the name Cuzens (Cussen or Cousins) recurs frequently in board reports and correspondence during the 1870s. There was a James Cousins still living at Framlingham, and he was there in 1885 when an *Argus* journalist visited the station. He mentioned 'Cozens, who was one of the Aboriginal team which went to England'. It is probable that the man in question was Mosquito, notable for his undistinguished tour of England. In the 1872 board report, there is mention of 'James Cousens, alias Mosquito'. His age was given as 25 years and his height as 5 feet 4 inches. In his undocumented essay on the tour, apparently based on *Scores and Biographies*, Pridham stated that Cuzens and Mosquito were brothers, and this seems to be confirmed by an obituary note on Cuzens.

Mosquito was more skilled as an artisan than as a cricketer. The Framlingham superintendent described him as 'remarkable for the ability with which he executes any piece of fancy work, especially in the way of carpentering'. He was also adept at making whips, an interesing link with his stock-whip act on tour. Perhaps most surprising of all his accomplishments was his apparent literacy, combined with a clear, firm hand. In June 1876 he wrote the following letter, apparently to a board official. (The contents of the letter make it unlikely that he had it written for him by a European and in any case there are other letters from Mosquito written in the same hand) (Figure F).

> I write to you with the intention of bringing under your notice that I have been working on the Station this last six years. And never received any payment for the same doing Carpenter work. And I wish to let you know if they intend giving me any thing for my work I would prefer a double barreled gun for the money. I have made a bullock dray wheel for the dray. Please write as soon as convenient.
>
> > I remain your true servant
> > James Cousins

But Mosquito was a man of many parts. In 1879 when an average number of 60 Aborigines lived at Framlingham, the superintendent reported a 'most earnest, successful and genuine religious revival' associated with a temperance campaign. The meetings lasted more than six weeks and were led by two Aborigines, including James Cussen. Except for a few recalcitrant old men, the two revivalists 'thoroughly aroused [the congregation] to their condition as sinners and their need of salvation'. Cussen's (Mosquito) only child, Sarah, died from tuberculosis in 1880, aged eight. It must be inferred from the records that he died between 1887 and 1890. Mosquito left no direct descendants, but Cousins is a name which survives in the Western District through his wife's subsequent family.[4]

'Tommy Redcap' appears in miscellaneous references in correspondence to the board. He later lived near the river at the small Dergholm reserve but at first he camped near Red Cap Creek, which bears his name today. In 1871, a local pastoralist benefactor wrote to the board seeking clothing for the few Aboriginal people there. Red Cap's clothing needs were given as those of a man five foot six inches tall and 'not stout'. They included blankets, flannel shirts, neck handkerchiefs, two pairs of trousers, two waistcoats and three felt hats. Red Cap still resided at Dergholm in 1879, when he sought a grant of 40 acres of land. He was commended by the local voluntary guardian of Aborigines as being steady and industrious. He had built a sound hut on the reserve lands and fenced in a garden. He and his wife, Caroline, were there in 1881 when he was again described as sober and reliable. During the shearing season he was fully employed as a shearer at standard European wages. Whenever he received his wages, he made a point of repaying the guardian for any food or clothing supplied to himself and Caroline.

Red Cap was well known as a shearer. At the Roseneath shed on 11 November 1881 he shore 91 sheep; his total for the season was 1274 sheep. Red Cap spent some time in the Hamilton Hospital during 1886, but recovered. He presumably lived in his cottage by the Glenelg River until his death, which probably occurred between 1891, when Hayman referred to him, and 1894. In that year the board relinquished its claim to the tiny Dergholm reserve, which passed into private ownership. It is likely that by this time the Red Cap family were the only tenants on the reserve. His grave is said to have been under a wattle tree just outside the Dergholm cemetery.[6]

Two European members of the original Bringalbert woolshed cricket team showed solicitude for ageing and displaced Aborigines. Hugh McLeod of Benayeo served the board as a local guardian of Aborigines for many years. A. A. Cowell of Brippick station, Booroopki, and later of Neuarpurr in the Apsley district, acted unofficially but with great compassion. It is evident that territorial bonds proved too strong for many Aborigines. Despite the official policy of concentrating these people on Aboriginal stations, they drifted away again to the lands of their birth. As a result, sympathetic settlers such as McLeod and Cowell sustained groups of dark people on their holdings, largely at their own expense. In the 1880s their charitable endeavours ran counter to the wishes of the board and Aboriginal station superintendents. Ageing cricketers were the beneficiaries of Cowell's generosity.

The irrepressible Jimmy Tarpot and his wife Jenny were listed as absentees from Ebenezer (Lake Hindmarsh) station in 1876. In 1879 Tarpot was playing cricket with the Harrow team, and in 1881 Tarpot and Jenny were living on Brippick. Cowell estimated their ages at 38 years and 40 respectively. Tarpot apparently returned to his traditional estates, and because of Cowell's sympathetic attitude he remained there. He died at Booroopki on 17 April 1900. Another cricketer possibly cared for by Cowell was Peter, described by him as an old man in 1881. The identification is tentative, because Peter was a common Aboriginal name. However, a 'Peter' was an absentee on the same 1876 Ebenezer list as that containing the Tarpots.[6]

Cowell also sustained Lake Billy, a member of the first Sydney touring side. In 1881 he reported that he had built a two-roomed house for Lake Billy, aged 50, and his lubra. They were there a year later; in 1884 Cowell observed that they were due back at his property after a visit to Naracoorte.[7]

Tiger was another team member known to Cowell, who stated that he had died before 1884. Perhaps Tiger's declining years were not as sheltered as those of Mosquito, Red Cap or Tarpot. An appendix to a board report lists those Aborigines committed to jails during 1874. Among these names is Harry Tiger, 'one of the Aboriginal cricketers taken to England'. He was charged with being drunk and disorderly at Sunbury, near Melbourne. Sadly, he continued a behavioural characteristic already manifest in England.

Harry Rose almost toured England, for he reached Geelong with Lawrence's men. He returned from Geelong in 1867, and by the following January he had been sentenced to jail for drunkenness by the Hamilton Court. Later board reports tell a sad story of 'drunk, and furious driving' in the gold-mining centre of Stawell, and drunken behaviour and larceny in several centres over as many years. He was a restless man and caused much dissension at Lake Condah station on periodic visits. With the new century, however, he reformed. He settled at Lake Condah, and at the mature age of 56 married Maryann Carmichael in April 1901. His wife died four years later, and he lived on at Condah until his death on 5 January 1916. He left no descendants[9] (Plate 30).

Another member of the abortive 1867 Sydney tour was Billy Officer. He was involved in a sly-grog charge in Edenhope during 1868. Four years later he and his wife were living at Lake Condah mision. His age in 1873 was estimated at 35. It must be inferred from the absence of his name from later records, in which Mrs Officer and her son Henry are involved, that Billy died at Lake Condah in 1874 or 1875.[10]

Charley Dumas may have remained in Sydney, because he did not play in the Melbourne game; his subsequent career is unknown. The other possible New South Wales team member, Twopenny, must have gravitated to Sydney, because he played there in an intercolonial match in 1870, representing New South Wales against Victoria. He could not recapture his devastating Hampshire form and failed to take a wicket in 30 overs, from which 56 runs were scored. He only made 8 runs with the bat in two innings. At this time, Harpur described him as 'a fast and straight bowler, with a good length and nip off the pitch'. Harpur admitted that some contended that he threw the ball, and cricketing writer C. P. Moody was one of these critics. If Twopenny's phenomenal English success resulted from a dubious delivery, he was the first 'chucker' to make an international tour. W. R. Glasson stated in 1950 that, as a youth, he remembered Twopenny. At this time, Twopenny was said to be an inveterate old drunkard, who acted as a gateman on a station in the Molong area, 250 kilometres west of Sydney. Some time before his death from dropsy on 12 March 1883, Twopenny joined a group of fringe-dwelling Aborigines living in West Maitland. Although he was described by a sympathetic local journalist as 'one of the finest looking and most intelligent aboriginals I ever saw', his death is a forlorn reflection on the neglect of black by white society. Twopenny died destitute, but in the company of his own outcast but caring community, in a shed near the West Maitland railway station. Only 15 years earlier he had been a national celebrity. Europeans judged him to be an old man, but he probably failed to reach his half century.[11]

Manly and cheerful Dick-a-Dick deserves a better record for posterity. However, he vanished back into his traditional bushland, the area in which he located the lost Duff children in 1864. McKenzie, an historian of the Kaniva district, recorded that Dick-a-Dick was seen at a race meeting on Mt Elgin station in 1884. Dick-a-Dick was relocated under another guise in 1971, by linguistic researcher Dr Luise Hercus. In taped conversations the Madi-madi Aboriginal elder Jack Long recalled youthful memories of that distinguished man, who then lived on the Murray River, especially around Euston and Mildura. Long last talked with him there in the mid-1890s and Dick-a-Dick probably died about that time. At this time he was known as Euston Billy. As King Billy (but, alternatively, as King Dick), he wore an inscribed brass 'kingplate', awarded as an administrative device by insensitive royalty-conscious white Australians to black Australians, whose traditional society never knew the institution of kingship. According to Jack Long, Dick-a-Dick worked as a drover, or fencer, on stations along the river. Although he often spoke of his English experiences, taciturn Jack Long simply recalled, 'he said it was all right there in England, and it was all right here'.

All Australians lost a link with Dick-a-Dick around 1982, when the Mt Elgin homestead was needlessly demolished. It was the first substantial house in the Nhill district, of drop-slab red gum construction. With its association with the Duff children saga and with Dick-a-Dick, it merited its listing on the Register of the National Estate, even though that was unable to save it for posterity.[12]

According to Jack Long, Jim Crow was a brother to

Dick-a-Dick, who associated with him along the river towns. Although Sundown is unrecorded after his arrival back in Hamilton at the end of 1868, Jim Crow experienced a subsequent violent life. The name was ubiquitously given to dark people, and there were possibly two men of that name in Western Victoria, both with police records. Dr Hercus recorded a tradition from Jack Long that Jim Crow was murdered by an Aborigine at Euston. Board reports for the 1870s indeed contain references to a rather violent Jim Crow, who was confined to the lock-up in Swan Hill and Echuca, both towns on that river. In 1876, a Jim Crow was listed as an absentee from Ebenezer station, then home to most of the people from Dick-a-Dick's territory. As a Jim Crow was arrested in Swan Hill during 1875, he may have been this absentee. It must have been around this period that he was murdered by two Aborigines for violating Aboriginal marriage rules.[13]

Another team member who drifted across the border may have been Bullocky. An unconfirmed tradition has his bulky but decayed frame begging beer money from spectators at the Corowa cricket ground.[14]

Despite his talents as an all-rounder, Johnny Mullagh never played intercolonial cricket. His reputation established after the English tour, he was appointed as a professional by the Melbourne Cricket Club. However, he preferred life in his own territory and did not remain long in Melbourne. In tandem with Cuzens, he was hired for 20 weeks during the 1869–70 season. He played in only six matches before ill health, or possibly low morale, resulted in his return to Harrow. In eight innings he scored 209 runs, with the highest score of 69 not out; he took 8 wickets for 300 runs from 278 balls. His batting average was the second highest of the team (34.5), so it is not surprising that he was named in the squad from which the Victorian team was to be selected for the intercolonial match against New South Wales. His illness and sudden return to Harrow eliminated him from consideration. Even so, his name was retained in the squad of 18 contenders during the following season (1870–71), but as the MCC did not hear from him, his name was dropped.

Mullagh had another hour of glory in 1879 when, as a member of the Victorian team, he played against the All-England XI captained by Lord Harris. During the 1878–79 season his outstanding play for the Harrow club placed his name again before the public. He headed the club batting averages (21) and his 3.5 bowling average also topped the list. His score of 64 against Hamilton drew praise.

Although against the English team, he bowled only 12 overs without success and scored 4 in his first innings, his 36 was the highest score in Victoria's second innings of 156. It held the innings together, against the slow bowling of the leading English player, Emmett, who dominated the English bowling that season. The *Australasian* praised Mullagh's 'graceful forward play and strong defence'.

Years later, Lord Harris recalled Mullagh as 'a very elegant bat'. A sympathetic crowd, perhaps remembering his past feats, subscribed £50 and a gold watch for his benefit. Possibly some also felt a tinge of conscience. A Royal Commission on Aborigines in Victoria ordered a systematic count of Aborigines, which indicated that, by 1877, the number of people of full Aboriginal descent in the State had dwindled to an estimated 774; recent population studies suggest that in the Western District alone there may have been 10 times that number only 45 years previously. Mullagh was one of the best known survivors of this ageing remnant of his race.

When Mullagh first returned from Melbourne early in 1870, he must have been dispirited. William Hayman wrote to the *Australasian* in April, to assure supporters that Mullagh's move from 'town to country has proved beneficial'. At that time he was living on Bringalbert station, under the patronage of Tom Hamilton. During March he played in the Apsley cricket team against Harrow, scoring 59 not out. He soon changed sides.

For many years until the 1890 cricket season, Mullagh was a respected member of the Harrow club, playing in the regional Murray Cup competition, which was established in 1864, around the period when Mullagh first played cricket. The four competing teams in this contest were Harrow, Hamilton, Coleraine and Casterton. Some of Mullagh's Harrow team-mates had been associated with the initial attempt to teach cricket to the Aborigines, and Tarpot was also a member of the 1879 team. Largely due to the efforts of Mullagh and his patrons, the Edgar family, Harrow dominated the competition during the 1880s. These were the years of Harrow's fleeting fame when, during the two boom decades before the depression of the 1890s, its population rose to 1000, and it boasted a fine sports oval and a brass band.

According to Edgar family tradition, one of Mullagh's favourite batting strokes of this period was somewhat unorthodox. Dropping on one knee to a fast rising ball, he would hold the bat over his shoulder and parallel to the ground. The ball would touch the blade and shoot high over the wicket-keeper's head to the boundary. Playing in a local match on 31 December 1871, Mullagh scored a century, and he made 92 on 21 February 1880 against the XXII from Pigeon Ponds. During the 1881–82 season his scores for Harrow were 110, 61, 10, 3, 6, 47 and 97. At the Harrow cricket club sports in 1881 he was sufficiently lithe to pitch a cricket ball for 98 yards.

Mullagh represented the Western District–Mount Gambier region in an 1884–85 competition staged on turf wickets in Adelaide. He was the sole representative of the Harrow club. Mullagh opened the batting in each of the five competition matches. He totalled 104 runs, and his average of 26 topped his team's batting averages. His best performance was against Norwood, when he carried his bat with 43 not out in his team's total of 116 (15 men a side). The merit of this innings was enhanced by the fact that George Giffen, the young Test bowler, bowled unchanged throughout the innings, capturing six wickets. Mullagh top scored, also, against North Adelaide. The feature of his innings of 25 was his 'remarkably good' defence[15] (Plate 33).

Mullagh was an excellent horseman and he also travelled round the sheds at shearing time. However, he normally lived alone as a rabbiter on Edgar's Pine Hill property, and it was here that his health declined during 1890. A. A. Cowell, who knew him in these later years, described him as 'humble, upright, quiet, retiring and civil'. He was also sensitive to racial discrimination. He had been offended by the colour bar at York. A. G. Moyes recounted a similar incident in Victoria when Mullagh deliberately hit a catch rather than continue playing against the Apsley team, whose captain had called him 'a nigger'. On another occasion when the Harrow team was playing at a coastal town, James Edgar was present when team members were ushered to their rooms at the inn. However, Mullagh was shown to a room across the yard by the stables, which the innkeeper judged to be good enough for 'the nigger'. Proud Mullagh left the premises and slept the night in the open.

Indeed, Mullagh was profoundly influenced by his English experience. This sensitive man, who had taken a dignified stand against intolerance at York, in later life turned the discrimination against himself. His acceptance of European values may be reflected in his decision to remain unmarried. With a reversed sense of racial discrimination he is said to have refused to marry a woman of his own race, while acknowledging as a fact of life that he could not expect any European woman to accept him. With a pathetic pride, Mullagh showed Tom Hamilton his English souvenirs and portraits, explaining 'this is a London lady' or 'this is a Devonshire lady'. In response to Tom's question why he did not marry, he answered, 'A white woman won't have me, Mr Tom, and I will never have a black one'.

James Edgar discovered Mullagh's body at his bush camp on 14 August 1891. The spot is known as 'Johnny's Dam' to this day. His funeral at the Harrow cemetery was an emotional ceremony. His bat and some stumps were buried with him and each Harrovian cricketer threw a sprig of blackberries and yellow flowers into the grave, symbolizing the club colours. The *Hamilton Spectator* co-ordinated efforts for a memorial fund collection which amounted to £37 and sentiment flowed through letters and poems addressed to the editor (Plate 37).

The modern highway bypasses Harrow, while Edenhope, the former frontier shanty town on Lake Wallace, is now the thriving shire centre. In the cemetery on a hill above Harrow hamlet, the wind sighs through the she-oaks. Mullagh's grave, with neat headstone inscription and iron railings, stands apart from the other graves. In the forlorn sports ground (the 'Mullagh Oval') where the fate of the Murray cup was decided, until recently there were large pine trees, planted there in Mullagh's time. Almost obscured beneath their branches was his memorial, erected with the subscription fund (Plate 36). In best Victorian taste, it is a pink granite obelisk, surmounted by an urn. Details of his birth and death are inscribed on the front of the monument; on one side is his tour average of 23.65 and on the other, his Murray Cup average of 45.7 over three seasons. In the old Mechanics' Institute there was a portrait of Mullagh, in which he stood against a romantic English countryside. Subsequent years witnessed further decay. Today, Mullagh's monument stands in forlorn isolation, as the fringing trees have been felled and his obelisk and the oval allowed to fall into neglect. A few years ago the Mechanics' Institute, erected in 1878 in Harrow' heyday, was destroyed by fire and Mullagh's portrait with it (Plate 32). By the time of the centenary of his death, all traces of his monument and oval may have been erased. It strengthens the case for placing the monument and his well-preserved grave on the Register of the National Estate. Fortunately, both the homesteads with which he was associated, Mullagh and Pine Hill, already are listed on that Register.[16]

Despite the havoc of time, however, and long after all memory of his team-mates has faded, Mullagh remains the dominant force in the folklore of this pastoral region. Some of these stories are recounted by Moyes in his discussion of the tour. They are not reproduced here because of their covert racism and implausibility.

The team is commemorated in Edenhope. On the lake foreshore where the team practised under Wills and Lawrence, the Edenhope High School stands today (Plate 38). Largely through the efforts of a master, Mr H. G. Martindale, a monument was set up on the school lawns. On it are inscribed the names of the 1868 team members. It was unveiled in 1951 by former Australian XI captain Victor Richardson. Since 1984 the team also has been commemorated at the MCG, by a bronze plaque.

The Europeans associated with the cricketers dispersed. Tom Hamilton died in 1872 and the family association with Bringalbert ceased a few years later. The Hayman family left Lake Wallace South in 1868 and at the time of Mullagh's death, William Hayman, JP was managing a pastoral property at Balmoral and was the energetic secretary of the Balmoral Pastoral and Agricultural Society. He married Sophie Leontine Constance Clarke in 1872 and they had four children. Hayman suffered from a spinal complaint for many years and shortly before his death, on 23 July 1899, he also had major surgery on his throat. He had become a popular community figure, active in the erection of the Anglican church, president of the Kowree Shire Council and 'esteemed for his urbanity and courtesy'. Whatever his managerial and business faults as a young man, therefore, he overcame them. Aged only 57 when he died, Hayman still outlived most of his team[17] (Plate 34).

Although he maintained a lifetime interest in his Mount Talbot property, C. M. Officer moved to Melbourne around 1872, at which time Aborigines were still employed on the station. His substantial mansion has been placed on the Register of the National Estate. Dr W. T. Molloy had left

Balmoral by 1871, but he continued his interest in Aboriginal affairs from his suburban Hawthorn practice. Tom Wills last played cricket in 1869 and he committed suicide in 1880, leaving his role in originating Australian Rules football as his chief Victorian memorial.

The two Sydney backers eventually resumed their accustomed activities. George Smith reappears in *Sands Sydney and Surburban Directory* from 1871, living at his previous address, Undercliffe, Belgrave Street, Manly, but by that date he was a Justice of the Peace. Smith still was a Manly resident at the time of his death, on 2 November 1889. Possibly G. W. Graham remained in England after the tour ended, as his name is absent from the *Directory* until 1875, when he resumed his solicitor's practice in Elizabeth Steet, Sydney, later moving to Bourke Street. His name no longer appeared as a practising solicitor by 1888.

Charles Lawrence evidently abandoned the Pier Hotel on Manly's Esplanade upon his departure for England. He had previously run a cricket goods shop and café at 353 George Street, Sydney. In search of greater security, after his return he joined the public service. Before his professional cricket career, he had worked as an assistant on a Scottish railway station. He returned to that profession in the New South Wales railways, working at Newcastle until his retirement at the age of 63. Lawrence continued to play cricket with the Newcastle Club, where he was known as 'the Old Master'. Between 1870 and 1872 he headed club batting averages and, in three memorable games against Maitland during 1871, he bowled unchanged through all three matches, capturing 31 wickets for 117 runs. His last cricketing appearance in New South Wales was in 1884, when he participated in a benefit match at the Sydney Cricket Ground and scored 31 runs. By this time his son, C. W. Lawrence, was a leading Newcastle batsman.

Lawrence moved to Melbourne around 1891, where he was engaged during eight seasons as coach to junior members of the Melbourne Cricket Club. His genial manner, ample grey beard and experience made him both a popular and successful coach to the colts. At the age of 70 he played his last game, scoring seven runs in 48 minutes at the crease. Young Vernon Ransford was a player who learned much from his example. During the last year of his life he started writing his brief memoirs, but he tired, unfortunately, at the high point of his career — when he arrived in England with the Aborigines. He died in 1917, aged 88. Two years later 91 years old William Caffyn died in England.

William Shepherd never played again for Surrey after 1868, but was appointed coach and groundkeeper at Dulwich College in 1872. He frequented the Oval in his declining years, retailing cricketing memories to patient bystanders. His nostalgic and not always accurate version of the Aboriginal tour was published in 1919, the year of his death.[18]

Dunstan concluded his account of the Aboriginal tour with a cynical observation: 'if only the tour had made money then there would have been interest in the Aboriginals as sportsmen'. There is merit in this provocative comment.[19] The widespread enthusiasm with which Aborigines played cricket during the 1870s and 1880s has been described. It should have been possible to direct this interest into a more systematic approach to the game. However, the players aged as the century neared its end, while European humanitarians became obsessed with the concept of 'smoothing the dying pillow' of the Aboriginal race. But, paradoxically, in this situation colonial governments did increasingly less for the welfare of fewer Aborigines.

Perhaps, also, by the turn of the century cricket lost its priority in the minds of white officialdom and paternalists as a suitable means of 'civilizing' the natives. In the first place, increasing numbers in south-eastern and south-western Australia were of mixed racial descent. By the laws of some States, Victoria included, convenient redefinitions classed such people as non-Aboriginal, thereby excluding them from living on established settlements and from receiving any related welfare benefits. Many potential black cricketers must have been so defined out of settlement teams.

Equally relevant was the apparent reality that, simply because Aborigines played good cricket and observed the rules of the game on the field, they were not transformed as a result into subservient gentlemen off the field. In England the cosy mythology about the equality of prince and peasant team members, publicized on belt buckles during the 1860s, never really applied once the peasant hitched up his working trousers with a different belt. The deference to social betters in the English scene was perpetuated in the Amateur–Professional distinction. Such concepts received less acceptance in the more egalitarian colonies. So it was that Jack might be as good as his captain, provided that he was white. It was a different matter when, during the 1880s, Bagot Morgan of Maloga Mission, near Echuca, appeared independent and showed 'ingratitude' to the superintendent after a successful cricket match against a European team.[20]

Possibly this Maloga experience provides a clue to the decline of Aboriginal cricket. The official policy on government settlements and missions alike was to concentrate Aboriginal people and to isolate them from contacts with the world outside. Cricketers, however, travelled around and gained the respect of their opponents, at the same time as gaining opportunities to drink alcohol. The Maloga missionary, who had promoted the sport, found his wandering cricketers to be 'proud' and 'subversive' and that 'their attitude [was] very trying, perplexing'. Cricket had succeeded too well as a social comforter and in forging some common bond between white and black players. Those officials who previously had promoted it no longer felt enthusiastic about its potential. They now wanted to segregate all persons of full Aboriginal descent, in the certainty that, when they became extinct, the Aboriginal 'problem' would be over.

Over the following century, a number of Aboriginal men and women have achieved prominence on the sporting arena, but their number on the cricket field is few. Most stars have enjoyed brief and controversial careers and the three most successful fast bowlers were all accused of 'chucking'. There are some who felt that it was their skin colour rather than an alleged offending throwing arm that was under criticism. There was a brief interlude during the Depression era when Eddie Gilbert (1906–78) became a legend. His 87 first-class wickets for Queensland included Bradman, then at the peak of his career. Another Queensland speedster, Albert Henry (1880–1909), represented his State seven times between 1901 and 1905. He came to public notice while playing with the Deebing Creek Aboriginal team. He contributed to sports history when he played against another Aboriginal representing another State. This was Jack Marsh (1872–1916), whose fast bowling took 34 wickets for New South Wales in six matches between 1901 and 1904. All three stars suffered criticism while celebrities and indignities once the public forgot them. Gilbert spent years in a mental home, while Marsh was murdered outside a pub in Orange and Henry was confined to Yarrabah mission station as he was considered by administrators to be unduly defiant of authority. Although on their records, all merited Test selection, they were overlooked. The only cricketer of acknowledged Aboriginal descent to represent Australia was Faith Thomas of Adelaide, who played as a bowler in the Australian women's cricket team.[21]

While Aboriginal boxers have been the subject of some scholarly research, a major project awaits attention in the sociology of Australian sport.[22] This is the role which sports of European origin have played in Aboriginal society, their differential regional adoption and adaptation, and the manner in which successful individual stars have thereby contributed to Aboriginal cultural identity in modern Australian society. A cynical scholar also might contrast the praises which white Australian society heaps upon Aboriginal sporting prowess, with the rapidity with which memories are erased and societal debts forgotten. The rise of the Aboriginal team to stardom in 1866–68 and its subsequent neglect offers a sad model.

Although recalled today only in dim folklore, no event in Aboriginal sporting history has rivalled the rapid rise of the Western District Aborigines to stardom and temporary acceptance in a racially conscious era. They departed for overseas only just in time. Probably because of their unorthodox exit from the colony, efforts were redoubled to prevent a recurrence of interference with 'welfare' policies. In Victoria, Brough Smyth and the Central Board for the Protection of the Aborigines finally engineered their necessary statutory authority, and this may have played its part in inhibiting further European speculation. The board, and the attorney-general, had been powerless to prevent the 1867 and 1868 tours leaving Victoria. Late in the following year they were granted the requisite powers. *An Act to Provide for the Protection and Management of the Aboriginal Natives of Victoria* (Victoria, number 349) was passed on 11 November 1869. It seems probable that the board influenced the framing of this legislation, particularly as the chief secretary had invited suggestions in his earlier correspondence with Brough Smyth over the cricketers. However, the chief secretary's records contain no further references to the Aboriginal cricketers, and in the debate on the Bill no speaker referred to them or used their experiences as a timely warning to legislators. Strangely also, the reports of the board covering 1867–69 make no mention of the cricketers.

This Act was framed with well-intentioned paternalism, but it was suffused with racial superiority. It has been observed that Aboriginal rights were so infringed 'that even the dignity of deciding their own fate seemed lost'.[23] The Act gave the governor extensive powers to prescribe areas where Aborigines 'or any tribe' could reside and to regulate contracts and other business agreements between European employers and Aborigines. It also prescribed how money due to Aborigines should be spent and entrusted the care of children to the board, not to their parents. Section 2 prescribed penalties 'if any person shall...remove or attempt to remove or instigate any other person to remove any aboriginal from Victoria without the written consent...of the Minister'. Comparable government action gave all colonial governments complete control over the lives and futures of all Aboriginal people.

Prospective promoters of further cricketing enterprises would need to overcome many administrative difficulties and smuggling was no longer a legal solution. If this legislation had been on the statute books two years earlier, Bullocky and his team-mates would not have taken the field at Lord's, 10 years before white cricketers turned the imperial combat into a ritual.

NOTES

[1] The Sydney match was reported in *S.M.H.*, 13 February 1869. 'Longstop's' opinion was expressed in *Aust.*, 27 February 1869, and the *Galatea* match was described in *Argus*, 3–4 March 1869. MCC financial terms, MCC Minute Book, 18 January 1869.

[2] The Hayman tribute, *H.S.*, 13 and 20 March 1869, and the Sundown news item *H.S.?* December 1868 and *Aust.* 19 December 1868.

[3] Hayman's letter was published in *H.S.*, 1 September 1891.

[4] Information concerning Cuzens is taken from MCC Minutes, 4, 15 October, 14 December 1869, 17, 18 February, 10 March 1870; R. C. Osburne, *The History of Warrnambool* (Melbourne, 1887), 205; Pridham, *Charm of Cricket*, 40; *Cricket Scores and Biographies*, vol 10, 413; report on death–*Bell's London*, 1 July 1871. Evidence for Mosquito also comes from *Scores and Biographies* and from *Report of the Board for the Protection of the Aborigines*, nos 8, 9, 15, and 17; *Argus*, 3 January 1885. The late Dr Diane Barwick directed our attention to much data, including records of the then Aborigines Welfare Board Office, Old Treasury Building, Melbourne. Cousins's letter is included in bundled In-letters from Framlingham. We are indebted to Mr P. E. Felton, at that time Superintendent of Aborigines Welfare, for permission to use this and subsequent data.

[5] Red Cap's career is based upon: In-letters, miscellaneous, Aborigines Welfare Board — from J. Ralston, 5 December 1879, and 13 September 1886; from Mary McDonald, 15 June 1881; M. Kiddle, *Men of Yesterday* (Melbourne, 1961), 302; L. J. Blake (ed), *Dergholm Centenary 1873–1973* (Penola, 1973), 8–9.

[6] Information on Tarpot: In-letters, miscellaneous, Aborigines Welfare Board — from Cowell, 27 February 1881, 2 July 1884; Aboriginal Register, held in 1965 by the Aborigines Welfare Board.

[7] For Lake Billy: In-letters, miscellaneous, Aborigines Welfare Board — from Cowell, 27 February 1881, 20 January 1882 and 27 September 1884.

[8] Data on Tiger: the letter from Cowell, 27 September 1884; *Report of the Board*, no 11, 23.

[9] Harry Rose: *Report of the Board*, nos 6, 7 and 37; personal communication from the late Dr Diane Barwick.

[10] Billy Officer: *Report of the Board*, no 10; *H.S.*, 5 February 1868; personal communication from the late Dr Diane Barwick.

[11] Twopenny: F. M. Harpur, 'Cricket footprints on the sands of time' (1932), unpublished MS notebooks in State Library of Victoria, La Trobe Library, Private Collections, Box 305/1, vol 1; C. P. Moody, *Australian Cricket and Cricketers* (Melbourne, 1894), 4, 33, 39; W. R. Glasson, *Yuranigh* (Sydney, n.d.), 22 — a reprint of a lecture delivered in Brisbane, 21 July 1950; J. Pollard, *Australian Cricket: The Game and the Players* (Sydney, 1983), 26, contains errors, but attributes his death to 1883. Obituary: *Maitland Mercury*, 15 March 1883, in sporting notes, by 'Vagrant'.

[12] Dick-a-Dick: F. K. McKenzie, *Back to Bill's Gully and Yanipy* (Kaniva, 1937), 3; Dr Luise Hercus, tape 3g2, side B, conversation with the late Jack Long, Point Pearce, 10 May 1971, A.I.A.S.; Mt Elgin homestead, *The Heritage of Australia* (Melbourne, 1981), sect 3/191.

[13] Jim Crow: Dr Luise Hercus, personal communication and the Jack Long tape, above; sundry references in Board *Reports*.

[14] Bullocky: MS of a talk by Mrs J. M. Boland at Balmoral, June 1969, courtesy of the late Mr C. Halahan, Edenhope.

[15] Mullagh: MCC Minutes, 4, 15 October, 14 December 1869, 17–18 February and Committee Report 1869–70 season; Moody, *Australian Cricket*, 54; Lord Harris, *A Few Short Runs* (London, 1921), 203. Western District population numbers are estimated at about 7900 by H. Lourandos, 'Aboriginal spatial organization and population', *Archaeology and Physical Anthroplogy in Oceania*, 12 (1977), 219. Hayman's

Comments: *Aust.*, 16 April 1870; Adelaide tour 1884–85: *Border Watch*, 3 January 1985.

[16] Cowell's judgement — *H.S.*, 27 August 1891. Racism: A. G. Moyes, *Australian Cricket: A History* (Sydney, 1959), 158; J. C. Hamilton, *Pioneering Days in Western Victoria* (Melbourne, 1912), 81. Mullagh's death evoked much nostalgia in *H.S.*, 15, 18, 20 and 22 August 1891. For the register of the National Estate listing of Pine Hill, Mullagh and Mount Talbot homesteads, see *The Heritage of Australia* (Melbourne, 1981), sect 3/191.

[17] Hayman's death: *H.S.*, 25 July 1899.

[18] W. Shepherd: *Wisden*, 1920, 185; his memoir was published in W. R. Weir (ed), *Ayre's Cricket Companion* (London, 1919), 128–34.

[19] K. Dunstan, *The Paddock that Grew* (Melbourne, 1962), 34.

[20] The Maloga model: Nancy Cato, *Mister Maloga* (St Lucia, 1976), 176–82.

[21] Later cricketers: J. Pollard, *Australian Cricket: The Game and the Players* (Sydney, 1983). Information about A. Henry, in unpublished thesis by Genevieve Blades (see Chapter 1).

[22] Aboriginal boxers have been discussed by Richard Broome, 'Professional Aboriginal boxers in eastern Australia 1930–1979', *Aboriginal History*, 4 (1980): 49–72. Also see Peter Corris, 'Black boxers', *Arena*, 37 (1975): 7–10, and *Lords of the Ring: A History of Prize-fighting in Australia* (Sydney, 1980).

[23] Comment on the Act: M. F. Christie, *Aborigines in Colonial Victoria 1835–86* (Sydney, 1979), 177.

Appendix I

Match 1   May 25–26 at the Oval *v*. Surrey
Surrey won by an innings and 7 runs
Surrey:	222	Mullagh 52 overs, 3 wickets, 100 runs
		Lawrence 49 overs, 7 wicket, 91 runs
Aborigines	83	Mullagh 33, King Cole 14
	132	Mullagh 73, Lawrence 22, Bullocky 19

Match·2   May 30 at Maidstone *v*. Maidstone
Match drawn
Maidstone:	151	Lord Paget 1; Lawrence 4/68
Aborigines:	119	for 4 wickets; Lawrence 57 n.o.,
		Tiger 21

Match 3   June 2–3 at Gravesend *v*. Gentlemen of Kent
Kent won by an innings and 69 runs
Kent:	298	Mullagh 59 overs, 6 wickets, 126 runs
Aborigines:	123	Dick-a-Dick 27, King Cole 18; Norton 5/2
	106	Red Cap 18, Mullagh 17

Match 4   June 5–6 at Deer Park *v*. Richmond
Match drawn
Richmond:	74	Cuzens 23 overs, 5 wickets, 28 runs
		Mullagh 15 overs, 3 wickets, 24 runs
	236	Mullagh 39 overs, 4 wickets, 65 runs
		Cuzens 36 overs, 3 wickets, 49 runs
Aborigines:	97	Cuzens 24, Tiger 19
	82	for 3 wickets; Lawrence 42 n.o.

Match 5   June 8–9 at Hove *v*. Sussex
Sussex won by 9 wickets
| Aborigines: | 171 | Lawrence 63, Mullagh 39 |
| | 89 | Lawrence 33, Mullagh 21 n.o. |

Sussex:	151	Mullagh 33 overs, 5 wickets, 55 runs
		Lawrence 25 overs, 3 wickets, 64 runs
	112	for 1 wicket

Match 6   June 10–11 at Ladywell *v.* Lewisham
Aborigines won by 6 wickets

Lewisham:	60	Mullagh 23 overs, 6 wickets, 24 runs
		Lawrence 22 overs, 3 wickets, 35 runs
	53	Mullagh 16 overs, 4 wickets, 20 runs
		Cuzens 12 overs, 3 wickets, 18 runs
Aborigines:	42	Red Cap 12
	72	for 4 wickets

Match 7   June 12–13 at Lord's *v.* MCC
MCC won by 55 runs

MCC:	164	Mullagh 45 overs, 5 wickets, 82 runs
		Cuzens 35 overs, 4 wickets, 52 runs
	120	Cuzens 35 overs, 6 wickets, 65 runs
		Mullagh 16 overs, 3 wickets, 19 runs
Aborigines:	185	Mullagh 75, Lawrence 31, sundries 31
	45	Cuzens 21, Mullagh 12

Match 8   June 15–16 at Southsea *v.* East Hampshire
East Hants won by an innings and 9 runs

East Hants:	209	Cuzens 43 overs, 6 wickets, 71 runs
Aborigines:	120	Mullagh 40, Bullocky 30
	80	Red Cap 23, Cuzens 17

Match 9   June 19–20 at Bishop's Stortford
Bishop's Stortford won by 8 wickets

Aborigines:	58	Mullagh 14
	99	Bullocky 25
B. Stortford:	136	Mullagh 28 overs, 6 wickets, 36 runs
		Cuzens 16 overs, 1 wicket, 33 runs
	23	for 2 wickets

Match 10   June 22–23 at Hastings
Match drawn

| Aborigines: | 119 | Cuzens 32, Mullagh 23 |
| | 185 | Mullagh 72, Bullocky 64 n.o. |

Hastings: 152   Mullagh 48 overs, 3 wickets, 47 runs
                       Cuzens 38 overs, 3 wickets 39 runs
           113   for 4 wickets

Match 11   June 26–27 at Halifax
Aborigines won by 7 wickets
Halifax: 64   Lawrence 30 overs, 6 wickets, 36 runs
                      Mullagh 31 overs, 4 wickets, 20 runs
          130   Mullagh 37 overs, 5 wickets, 35 runs
                      Lawrence 26 overs, 3 wickets, 53 runs
Aborigines: 166   Mullagh 56, Cuzens 42, Red Cap 33
           29   for 3 wickets

Match 12   June 29–30 at Blackburn *v*. East Lancashire
Match drawn
East Lancs: 234   Mullagh 42 overs, 6 wickets, 84 runs
            6   for 1 wicket
Aborigines: 144   Mullagh 41, Lawrence 25
          97   Bullocky 24, Lawrence 17

Match 13   July 2–3–4 at Rochdale
Rochdale won by 77 runs
Rochdale: 105   Mullagh 7 wickets, 58 runs
          91   Mullagh 35 overs, 5 wickets, 36 runs
                      Lawrence 30 overs, 2 wickets, 27 runs
Aborigines: 27
          92   Mullagh 23

Match 14   July 6–7 at Swansea *v*. South Wales
Aborigines won by an innings and 33 runs
South Wales: 68   Mullagh 26 overs, 5 wickets, 17 runs
                      Lawrence 25 overs, 4 wickets, 38 runs
          92   Mullagh 34 overs, 4 wickets, 23 runs
                      Lawrence 22 overs, 4 wickets, 40 runs
Aborigines: 193   Cuzens 50, Red Cap 37, Mullagh 25

Match 15   July 10–11 at Bradford
Match drawn
Bradford: 154   Cuzens 14 overs, 4 wickets, 21 runs
          16   for 1 wicket

Aborigines: 40
171 Mullagh 55, Twopenny 32, Tiger 23

Match 16   July 13-14 at York *v.* Yorkshire
Yorkshire won by an innings and 51 runs
Aborigines: 92 Cuzens 32
58 Cuzens 42
Yorkshire: 201 Red Cap 21 overs, 7 wickets, 34 runs

Match 17   July 16-17-18 at Manchester *v.* Longsight
Longsight won by 4 wickets
Aborigines: 53 Cuzens 10
123 Lawrence 37, Cuzens 31
Longsight: 78 Lawrence 21 overs, 5 wickets, 49 runs
Mullagh 21 overs, 4 wickets, 26 runs
100 Mullagh 23 overs, 3 wickets, 38 runs

Match 18   July 20-21 at Bury
Match drawn
Bury: 99 Mullagh 33 overs, 5 wickets, 35 runs
Lawrence 36 overs, 3 wickets, 42 runs
93 Lawrence 34 overs, 6 wickets, 62 runs
Mullagh 35 overs, 4 wickets, 23 runs
Aborigines: 53 Twopenny 23
128 for 5 wickets; Mullagh 49

Match 19   July 23-24 at Norwich *v.* Carrow Club
Aborigines won by an innings and 52 runs
Carrow: 82 Lawrence 26 overs, 4 wickets, 57 runs
Mullagh 26 overs, 4 wickets, 18 runs
101 Lawrence 35 overs, 8 wickets, 50 runs
Aborigines: 235 Cuzens 87, Mullagh 42

Match 20   July 27-28 at Keighley, Yorkshire
Match drawn
Keighley: 118 Red Cap 24 overs, 5 wrickets, 54 runs
146 Lawrence 28 overs, 7 wickets, 54 runs
Aborigines: 101 Lawrence 28
142 for 8 wickets; Cuzens 70

Match 21   July 30–31–August 1 at Liverpool *v*. Bootle
Aborigines won by 9 wickets
Bootle: 110   Lawrence 32 overs, 5 wickets, 62 runs
                          Red Cap 32 overs, 4 wickets, 37 runs
                   90   Lawrence 15 overs, 5 wickets, 26 runs
Aborigines: 115   Lawrence 50 n.o., Dick-a-Dick 22
                   87   for 1 wicket; Cuzens 54 n.o.

Match 22   August 3–5 at Trent Bridge *v*. Nottingham
Match drawn
Nottingham: 91   Mullagh 29 overs, 4 wickets, 56 runs
                          Lawrence 29 overs, 5 wickets, 57 runs
                   372   Cuzens 51 overs, 5 wickets, 82 runs
Aborigines: 76   Cuzens 43
                   57   for 4 wickets

Match 23   August 7–8 at Manchester *v*. Longsight
Aborigines won by 107 runs
Aborigines: 75   Mullagh 25
                   151   Mullagh 33, Twopenny 29
Longsight: 47   Mullagh 15 overs, 6 wickets, 18 runs
                          Lawrence 15 overs, 3 wickets 25 runs
                   72   Lawrence 23 overs, 8 wickets, 48 runs

Match 24   August 10–11 at Bramhall Lane *v*. Sheffield
Match drawn
Sheffield: 133   Lawrence 37 overs, 4 wickets, 86 runs
                          Mullagh 49 overs, 6 wickets, 95 runs
Aborigines: 185   Mullagh 55, Twopenny 22

March 25   August 13–14–15 at Dewsbury *v*. Savile
Savile won by an innings and 58 runs
Savile: 217   Lawrence 58 overs, 6 wickets, 96 runs
Aborigines: 73   Tiger 20
                   86   Mullagh 48

Match 26   August 17–18 at North Shields *v*. Tynemouth
Aborigines won by 2 wickets
Tynemouth: 54   Mullagh 23 overs, 4 wickets, 24 runs
                          Lawrence 23 overs, 4 wickets, 26 runs

	144	Mullagh 5 wickets, 67 runs
Aborigines:	35	Mullagh 17
	166	for 8 wickets; Cuzens 59

Match 27   August 21–22 at Newcastle v. Northumberland
Match drawn

Northumber-land:	162	Lawrence 36 overs, 5 wickets, 89 runs
		Cuzens 22 overs, 4 wickets, 28 runs
Aborigines:	72	
	31	for 3 wickets

Match 28   August 24–25 at Middlesbrough
Match drawn

Middles-brough:	151	Red Cap 22 overs, 5 wickets, 32 runs
	78	Lawrence 23 overs, 6 wickets, 48 runs
Aborigines:	74	
	77	for 9 wickets; Lawrence 35 n.o.

Match 29   August 27–28–29 at Scarborough
Aborigines won by 10 wickets

Scarborough:	90	Cuzens 18 overs, 4 wickets, 23 runs
	109	Lawrence 38 overs, 6 wickets, 54 runs
Aborigines:	148	Red Cap 56, Mullagh 39
	53	for no wicket; Twopenny 35 n.o.

Match 30   August 31–September 1 at Leeds v. Hunslet
Aborigines won by 7 wickets

Hunslet:	71	Mullagh 18 overs, 5 wickets, 27 runs
	18	Lawrence 14 overs, 5 wickets, 10 runs
		Mullagh 14 overs, 4 wickets, 7 runs
Aborigines:	64	
	26	for 3 wickets

Match 31   September 2–3 at Derby v. South Derbyshire
South Derbyshire won by 139 runs

South Derby:	121	Lawrence 30 overs, 6 wickets, 67 runs
		Mullagh 28 overs, 3 wickets, 46 runs
	125	Mullagh 31 overs, 4 wickets, 40 runs
Aborigines:	76	Twopenny 33; J. Smith 6/28
	31	J. Smith 6/16

Match 32   September 4–5 at Lincoln
Lincoln won by 10 runs

Lincoln:	44	Mullagh 22 overs, 6 wickets, 23 runs
		Lawrence 23 overs, 4 wickets, 20 runs
	100	Mullagh 41 overs, 5 wickets, 42 runs
		Cuzens 33 overs, 4 wickets, 30 runs
Aborigines:	78	Lawrence 37
	56	

Match 33   September 7–8 at Burton-on-Trent
Aborigines won by 69 runs

Burton:	72	Lawrence 14 overs, 5 wickets, 29 runs
		Cuzens 23 overs, 4 wickets, 18 runs
	99	Lawrence 24 overs, 7 wickets, 47 runs
Aborigines:	139	Mullagh 42, Red Cap 25
	101	Lawrence 42; Bass 5/46

Match 34   September 10–11–12 at Liverpool *v.* Bootle
Aborigines won by 154 runs

Aborigines:	148	Mullagh 51, Peter 30
	156	Mullagh 78, Cuzens 28
Bootle:	91	Mullagh 25 overs, 7 wickets, 32 runs
	59	Mullagh 16 overs, 4 wickets, 17 runs
		Lawrence 17 overs, 5 wickets, 37 runs

Match 35   September 14–15 at Witham
Aborigines won by an innings and 43 runs

Aborigines:	184	Cuzens 64, Lawrence 48
Witham:	82	Mullagh 27 overs, 5 wickets, 27 runs
		Cuzens 7 overs, 3 wickets, 5 runs
	59	Lawrence 20 overs, 7 wickets, 33 runs
		Mullagh 17 overs, 3 wickets, 18 runs

Match 36   September 17–18 at Brighton *v.* Sussex
Match drawn

Aborigines:	96	Lawrence 55
	113	for 7 wickets; Tiger 32
Sussex:	74	Lawrence 23 overs, 6 wickets, 33 runs

Match 37   September 21–22 at Blackheath
Blackheath won by 13 runs
Blackheath: 121   Lawrence 29 overs, 3 wickets, 45 runs
                 75   Red Cap 22 overs, 3 wickets, 29 runs
                      Cuzens 5 overs, 3 wickets, 1 run
Aborigines: 67   Bullocky 15
                116   Mulagh 36

Match 38   September 23–24 at Islington *v.* Middlesex
Match drawn
Middlesex: 105   Mullagh 26 overs, 6 wickets, 45 runs
                175   Lawrence 20 overs, 5 wickets, 62 runs
Aborigines: 163   Cuzens 66, Mullagh 35

Match 39   September 26 at the Oval *v.* Surrey
Match drawn
Surrey: 175   Lawrence 33 overs, 5 wickets, 72 runs
Aborigines: 24   for 3 wickets

Match 40   September 28–29 at Maidstone *v.* the Press
Match drawn
Press: 101   Lawrence 28 overs, 6 wickets, 45 runs
                      Mullagh 17 overs, 3 wickets, 29 runs
                 74   Cuzens 9 overs, 4 wickets, 16 runs
                      Mullagh 21 overs, 3 wickets, 15 runs
Aborigines: 82   Mullagh and Cuzen 21

Match 41   September 30–October 1 at Eastbourne
Match drawn
Eastbourne: 67   Cuzens 22 overs, 6 wickets, 19 runs
                      Red Cap 12 overs, 4 wickets, 10 runs
                 94   Red Cap 18 overs, 5 wickets, 34 runs
Aborigines: 70   Mullagh 35

Match 42   October 2–3 at Hammersmith *v.* Turnham Green
Match drawn
Turnham
Green: 62   Mullagh 19 overs, 5 wickets, 26 runs
Aborigines: 48

Match 43   October 5–6 at Southsea *v*. East Hampshire
Aborigines won by an innings and 72 runs
East Hants: 51   Twopenny 10 overs, 9 wickets, 9 runs
                22   Twopenny 16 overs, 6 wickets, 7 runs
Aborigines: 144   Lawrence 35, Bullocky 34

Match 44   October 7–8 at Southampton *v*. Hampshire
Match drawn
Hampshire: 53   Twopenny 21 overs, 9 wickets, 17 runs
             152   Twopenny 17 overs, 3 wickets, 39 runs
                 Lawrence 27 overs, 4 wickets, 58 runs
Aborigines: 78   Cuzens 26
              49   for 3 wickets

Match 45   October 9–10 at Reading
Aborigines won by an innings and 218 runs
Reading: 32   Mullagh 7 overs, 8 wickets, 9 runs
              34   Lawrence 8 overs, 8 wickets, 9 runs
                 Red Cap 7 overs, 5 wickets, 10 runs
Aborigines: 284   Mullagh 94, Cuzens 66, Bullocky 37

Match 46   October 12–13–14 at Godalming
Match drawn
Godalming: 37   Lawrence 6 wickets, 18 runs
            128   Lawrence 4 wickets, 52 runs
Aborigines: 79   Cuzens 20
              25   for 6 wickets

Match 47   October 15–16–17 at the Oval *v*. Surrey
Surrey won by 9 wickets
Aborigines: 56   Bullocky 24
            143   Cuzens 63, Red Cap 22
Surrey: 173   J. C. Gregory 121 n.o.
              29   for 1 wicket

Appendix II

Batting

Name	Matches Played	Completed Innings	Times Not Out	Total	Highest Score	Average
Mullagh	45	71	4	1,698	94	23.65
Lawrence	40	57	12	1,156	63	20.16
Cuzens	46	72	8	1,358	87	19.9
Bullocky	39	61	3	579	64	9.33
Red Cap	47	73	3	630	56	8.46
Twopenny	46	70	6	589	35	8.29
King Cole	7	10	2	75	18	7.5
Tiger	47	69	5	431	32	6.17
Shepherd	7	11	0	66	11	6.0
Dick-a-Dick	45	66	5	356	42	5.26
Peter	42	59	7	284	30	4.48
Charley	44	53	13	218	17	4.6
Mosquito	34	20	26	77	8	3.17
Jim Crow	13	15	4	37	12	2.7
Sundown	2	3	0	1	1	—

* These figures are adapted from the *Sporting Life*, 28 October 1868.

Bowling

Name	Overs	Maidens	Runs	Wickets	Average
Twopenny	176	78	242	35	6.9
Mullagh[†]	1,877	831	2,489	245	10.0
Red Cap	366	141	576	54	10.7
Cuzens	868	361	1,296	114	11.3
Bullocky	22	7	46	4	11.5
Lawrence[†]	1,579	451	3,022	250	12.1
Dick-a-Dick	35	6	96	5	19.2
Shepherd	56	14	124	6	20.7
King Cole	14	4	34	1	—

All overs were four-ball.
    [†] This analysis does not include figures for the first innings against Rochdale, and the second innings against Tynemouth (North Shields), when Lawrence took 7 wickets and Mullagh 12. Both bowlers would have taken 257 wickets in this case.

Appendix III

No claim to total reliability is possible because of the scrappy nature of sources.

Date	Opponents, venue	Result
FIRST TOUR 1866		
24 January	Edenhope at Bringalbert	W
March	Hamilton	W
March	Balmoral	L
December	L. Wallace	L
December	L. Wallace (16)	W
December	L. Wallace (16)	W
26–27 December	Melbourne Cricket Club	L
1867		
4–5 January	Corio club, Geelong	W
11–12 January	Prince of Wales, Collingwood (15)	W
18–19 January	Bendigo	W
29 January	Yarra Yarra, Heidelberg (18)	D
31 January	Ballarat	L
8–9 February	County of Bourke, MCG	W
21–22 February	Albert Club, Redfern	L
1–3 March	Maitland	L

Aborigines	Opponents	Features
36/26	75	
36/30	64/59	Mullagh 5 wickets
98/1 for 38	75/59	Mullagh 31
34	8 for 170	Mullagh 81; 6 wickets
95 in 2 ins.	164	
101/1 for 27	39/87	Cuzens 6 wickets; Mullagh 33
25/37	170	Mullagh 49; Bullocky 32.
81	130	Mullagh 50; Wills 49 and 10 wickets.
100/49	84/7 for 66	Wills 27; Mullagh 19.
102	2 for 8	
108/0 for 7	42/71	Cuzens 26; Wills 12 wickets
151/70	154/134	Cuzens 49 and 4 wickets.
135/163	72/92	
82/101	53/33	

Date	Opponents, venue	Result
4 March	Newcastle	D
12 March	Albert Club (seconds, 15)	W
16 March	Manly Beach	W
18 March	Albert club, Redfern	W
5–6 April	Wollongong	W
9–10 April	Parramatta	L
22–23 April	XI of NSW Redfern	L
9 May	Portland (17)	W

SECOND TOUR

Date	Opponents, venue	Result
28 August	Edenhope	W
2–3 October	Warrnambool (16)	W
5 October	Mortlake	D
10–11 October	Corio, Geelong	D
18–19 October	Corio, Geelong	D
6–7 November	Wollongong	W
11 November	West Maitland	W
14 November	Singleton	W
15–16 November	Newcastle	W
26 December	Bathurst	L

Aborigines	Opponents	Features
62/55	32/2 for 14	Dick-a-Dick 14
146	130	
83/2 for 63	53/89	Cuzens 11 wickets; Mullagh 50; Dick 29
131	129	Mullagh 75; Cuzens 6 wickets.
116	20	Mullagh 45
63/63	79/51	
90/37	99/43	Cuzens 20
100	43	Mullagh 7 wickets; Cuzens 5 wickets.
174	47	
140	17/26	Mullagh 48 and 10 wickets; Cuzens 6 wickets.
5 for 25	40	
64	69	
64/73	37/4 for 29	
86/2 for 45	27/102	Mullagh 7 wickets; Red Cap 18.
84/2 for 43	64/62	Mullagh 20 and 5 wickets.
48/0 for 14	25/36	Mullagh 10 wickets; Lawrence 10 wickets.
34/1 for 23	40/15	Mullagh, Cuzens 6 wickets each.
46/48	90/60	

Date	Opponents, venus	Result
1868		
4–5 February	Army & Navy, Redfern	D
RETURN 1869		
12 February	NSW Redfern	D
20–23 February	MCC	D
2 March	*Galatea* Officers	D

Aborigines	Opponents	Features
237	64/51 for 3	Cuzens 86; Mullagh 56; Bullocky 39; Cuzens 8 wickets.
	5 for 61	Match abandoned.
141/7 for 100	237	Mullagh 31; Twopenny 32
9 for 331	5 for 293	Cuzens 63; Twopenny 56; Red Cap 36.

Appendix IV

From the 1867 scorebook, *Sydney Morning Herald*, 12 February 1869 and *Sporting Life*, 16 May 1868.

European name	Traditional name	Variants
Bullocky	Bullchanach	Bullchanah
Cuzens (Cousins)	Yellanach	Zellanach, Zellemach
Dick-a-Dick	Jumgumjenanuke	Jungunjinanuke
Dumas (Charley)	Pripumuarraman	Brippohei
Jellico	Unamurrimin	
Jim Crow	Lytejerbillijun	
Lake Billy	Mijarrle	
Mosquito	Grongarrong	Grougarrong, Jarrawak
Mullagh	Unaarrimin	Muarrinim, Unarrimin
Officer, Billy	Cungewarrimim	
Paddy	Pappinjurumun	
Peter	Arrahmunyarrimun	Arrahmunijarrimun
Redcap	Brimbunyah	Britabunyah
Rose, C.	Bripumyarrimin	Brippoki, Brippokei
(King Cole)		
Rose, Harry	Hingingairah	
Sundown	Ballrinjarrimin	
Tarpot	Murrumgunerrimin	
Tiger	Bonnibarngeet	Bonmbarngeet, Bonnibarugeet
Twopenny	Jarrawuk	Bynyarra, Murrumgunarrimin
Watty	Bilayarrimin	

Appendix V

There are entries for each match of the tour, recording receipts and expenses. In a few instances expenses were paid during one match which might be recorded more properly against the whole tour. Table A summarizes receipts and expenditure throughout the tour, rounded to the nearest pound.

It is not possible to produce a complete dissection of finances because some entries either are incomplete or provide insufficient detail. Accordingly, the analysis provided in Table B includes some personal judgements. It classifies expenditure into Team and Match expenses, then further details are provided within these categories, including unusual items or ones difficult to allocate to the two major groupings.

From the data in Table A it is possible to calculate the accumulated surplus from the tour on a weekly basis. The surplus passed £1000 within four weeks and by match 23 it had reached £1700. The second half of the tour proved only one-third as profitable, producing only £500 surplus.

These contrasting fortunes become even more evident when they are set against the strains imposed on the team. At the start of the tour 14 players were available, but the tourists were reduced to 11 regulars by mid-tour. Rest days (excluding Sunday) also were reduced from 10 to four during the second half. With hindsight, it would have proved prudent to have halved the tour's duration.

TABLE A

Receipts, expenses and surpluses match-by-match (figures rounded to nearest pound)

Match	Venue	Receipts	Expenditure	Surplus	Deficit	Cumulative Surplus
1	The Oval	603	294	309		309
2	Maidstone	35	19	16		25
3	Gravesend	190	75	115		440
4	Richmond	161	77	84		524
5	Hove	235	67	168		692
6	Lewisham	85	27	58		750
7	Lord's	138	32	106		856
8	Southsea	114	76	38		894
9	Bishop's Stortford	144	95	49		943
10	Hastings	217	104	113		1056
11	Halifax	92	38	54		1110
12	Blackburn	144	89	55		1165
13	Rockdale	139	80	59		1224
14	Swansea	142	98	44		1268
15	Bradford	115	50	65		1333
16	York	68	52	16		1349
17	Manchester	208	158	50		1399
18	Bury	85	41	44		1443
19	Norwich	53	43	10		1453
20	Keighley	122	87	35		1488
21	Liverpool	228	81	147		1635
22	Nottingham	210	117	93		1728
23	Manchester	40	65		25	1703
24	Sheffield	218	108	110		1813
25	Dewsbury	48	46	2		1815
26	North Shields	66	74		8	1807
27	Newcastle	35	32	3		1810
28	Middlesborough	39	45		6	1804
29	Scarborough	174	107	67		1871
30	Leeds	60	37	23		1894

Match	Venue	Receipts	Expenditure	Surplus	Deficit	Cumulative Surplus
31	Derby	61	45	16		1910
32	Lincoln	102	64	38		1948
33	Burton on Trent	104	54	50		1998
34	Liverpool	86	88		2	1996
35	Witham	120	25	95		2091
36	Brighton	100	72	28		2109
37	Blackheath	91	74	17		2136
38	Islington	82	52	30		2166
39	The Oval	62	23	39		2295
40	Maidstone	27	113		86	2119
41	Eastbourne	82	50	32		2151
42	Turnham Green	5	8		3	2148
43	Southsea	6	24		18	2130
44	Southampton	51	24	27		2157
45	Reading	40	29	11		2168
46	Godalming	109	42	67		2235
47	The Oval	64	32	32		2267
48	Plymouth	16	91		75	2192
	TOTALS	5416	3224	2415	223	2192

TABLE B

Tour expenses directed according to team and match expenses

	£	%
Team expenses		
Travel	366	11.35
Accommodation	667	20.69
Meals	153	4.75
Upkeep, repairs, etc.	22	0.68
Incidentals	188	5.83
Total team expenses	1396	43.30
Match expenses		
Share of takings paid to other clubs	1143	35.45
Ground officials	44	1.37
Police, bands, etc.	90	2.79
Equipment	12	0.37
Printing and advertising	373	11.57
Prize money	102	3.17
Other match expenses	23	0.71
Total match expenses	1787	
Other expenses	41	1.27
Total	3224	100.00

Abbreviations

Accounts	G. W. Graham Ledger
Aust.	*Australasian* (Melbourne)
H.S.	*Hamilton Spectator*
Roch. Obs.	*Rochdale Observer*
S.M.H.	*Sydney Morning Herald*

Index